SOUL PURPOSE

YOUR SOUL PURPOSE

The 5 Elements to Discovering Your Purpose and Living the Life of Your Dreams

Have an enjoyable trip with this one. I'm not sure if I'm any the illuminated because of it but it gave me plenty to think about

By Brendan Nichols

Pamela.

Published by Avargo Press

Suite A, 23 Wirree Drive
Ocean Shores 2483
Australia

The examples within this book are based on true case histories. The names have been changed to protect the identities of the people involved.

DISCLAIMER
The author of this book does not dispense medical advice or prescribe the use of any technique as a form of treatment for physical, mental, emotional or medicinal problems without the advice of a physician, either directly or indirectly.
The exercises within this book have been used without any adverse affect in workshops and seminars, however the reader assumes full responsibility if using any of the information or exercises.
The intent of the author is only to offer information of a general nature to help you in your quest for emotional well-being and good health. In the event you use any of the information in this book for yourself, which is your constitutional right, the author and the publisher assume no responsibility for your actions.

The National Library of Australia Cataloguing-in-Publication entry

Nichols, Brendan.
Your soul purpose : the 5 elements to discovering your purpose and living the life of your dreams.

ISBN 0 646 41270 1.

1. Typology (Psychology). 2. Personality. 3. Self-actualization (Psychology). I. Title.

155.26

For information on distribution phone 612 9977 5064
or www. brendannichols.com
Printed in Australia by Griffin Press

ACKOWLEDGEMENTS

I am deeply grateful to the people who have assisted me in the process of this book. No one person is an island. This book began in the 1970's when I began in earnest my personal and spiritual journey. It would not have been possible without the loving support of all my teachers in the field of personal and spiritual development. My deepest thanks to each and every one of you. Thank you to Robert Kiyosaki, Vince and Yve Betar, Daria Peck, Diamond and River Jamieson, Al Running, Richard Running Deer, Pak Jero Sumadi, the writings of Carl Jung and his followers, the spiritual Teachers of India and many others. To my wife Annie, my most profound gratitude for your advice, support and love in our journey together. To my children who have enriched my life and my Mother and Father who laid such a wonderful foundation for me. To my brother Lucas and Colleen Nichols for being the great people that you are.

Thank you to the countless people who have promoted my work over the years and my many friends. To: David Zeltner, Robert Matthews and Dianne McCann. To Kim Hanlon and Patrick Burgess for a friendship spanning more than 30 years,Wayne and Lynn Morgan, Blair and Eileen Singer, Andrew and Kimberley Pollis, Wendy Gogerley, Bob and Collette Hemmenger, Denis Cooney, Denis Fountaine, Chris Disspain, Yehuda Bichler, David Balfour and Bridgett Benary, Kisha Burlinson and Alan Lauer, Dean and Heather Evans, Peter Johnston and Suzi Dafnis, Lianna de Steffano, James Caldwell, Krystyna Spicer, Pauline Abel, Terrence Michaels, Michelle Stevens, Tony and Carol Fogarty, Wayne and Raewyn, Ruth Tai, John Glover, Bob and Kelly, Michael and Wendy Keane, Suzi Balmer, Graham Harvey, Sean Knight for your diagrams, Mark Donaldson for the photos, Don Wareing and the WA crew,
and a host of other people.

I would like to thank:

Laurel Cohn, my editor, for your tremendous professionalism and suggestions in the design and text.

Special thanks to Tony and Jeanette Brenz-Verca, Kim Kiyosaki, John Harricharanim, Tim Wise, Jim and Colleen Nichols and Bob Erdman for your valuable assistance.

Lastly I want to thank the thousands of people who have attended my seminars. I have learned so much from you.

DEDICATION

To Annie and all those people who are bound by the common goal of the evolution of the human spirit.

If you wish to seek greatness
look in only one direction.
Closer than your own breath
nearer than your own skin.
Inside yourself is the blueprint
to freedom.

Brendan Nichols

Contents

PART ONE

THE SECRET THAT SHAPES DESTINY

PART TWO

THE FIVE ELEMENTS

The Visionary Leader

The Poet

The Sage

Spirit

PART THREE

AWAKENING THE ELEMENTS

PART ONE

THE SECRET THAT SHAPES DESTINY

PART ONE

THE CATALYST FOR THE SEARCH

What a blessed life. I have a beautiful, loving family; I live within earshot of the Pacific Ocean, with a tropical, emerald green rainforest and river in my backyard. I spend my time doing what I love — travelling the world and working with people who want to be successful in their careers and relationships, and who want to experience a deep sense of purpose and spiritual peace.

As I sit here today looking over my computer keyboard into the forest, I feel a tremendous inner peace and contentment. But it wasn't always that way. There was another day, in another time when I felt anything but peaceful.

It was the most horrific moment of my life. I was sitting on the sandstone rock next to the path that led up to our house, gazing out to sea. The wind was whipping in from the south-east, and the whole ocean was covered in whitecaps. Overhead, the sky was steel grey and overcast. My mood was pretty bleak as my wife and I had just had another harrowing disagreement that had left us standing in the lounge room, barely able to see each other around the mountain of misunderstandings that stood between us. We had been experiencing serious problems in our marriage for six months now, and I felt I was sinking in quicksand. No matter what I did, things only seemed to get worse.

As I sat there lost in my own thoughts, my wife came down the steps and quietly sat next to me. I turned towards her and could see that her beautiful face was set in an implacable mask.

She looked at me and said with complete conviction, "It's over. I'm not doing this anymore."

I knew her well enough to know that her decision was final. Our journey together was finished.

Suddenly, the ocean, her face and the entire surroundings took on a strange, surreal quality. Everything moved in slow motion and I felt as if I was drowning. I couldn't speak, I just sat there in shock. A feeling of utter loneliness enveloped me. I had always believed we would be married for ever. My family, the most important thing in my life, seemed to be vanishing before my eyes.

Up until that moment I had never really had an experience that had completely bowled me over. I was successful and had my own business. Deep down I thought something like this could never happen to me. People would tell me about traumatic experiences, but I never really understood. How can you unless you've been there?

That tumultuous event happened over 13 years ago and was the trigger for a profound personal transformation. As I look back on myself at that time and think about the person I am today, the two people seem totally different, like strangers.

What was it that created the change?

Prior to my marriage breaking up I had spent many years researching methods of attaining personal and spiritual potential. Right from my early teenage years I had always felt there was more to life than just existing. I sensed there was some grand purpose, that somehow everyone — including myself — was living a tiny fraction of their potential. From my youthful vantage point it seemed as though we had all forgotten some great secret and were immersed in our own bubble, rushing endlessly towards seemingly important things but somehow unaware of what was really meaningful. It was as if we were all working on some giant machine, with each one of us diligently working on one small part of the machine, but no one knowing what the whole machine actually did, or what it was for. We had lost the manual explaining how it worked.

I believe the book you are holding now is that manual.

After leaving school I spent years devouring hundreds of books. I studied most of the known motivational and success literature. I pored over many of the ancient texts of India and travelled there in 1976 to study meditation techniques. Over the years I researched dozens of cutting edge modalities in the field of psychology and human awareness. I had a very simple strategy. I would find someone who was a master in their field and then study with them in depth. I was passionately searching and the search was driven by two things: I wanted to improve myself and I wanted to find techniques that really worked. I wanted results.

I found early on that I had a talent for getting right to the core of a particular modality. I seemed to be able to grasp the very heart of the matter in a short period of time and transfer that into my life. I would throw myself into a particular field like a man possessed, sucking the very marrow out of a specific philosophy. Often my teachers, seeing my rapid progress, would encourage me to gain a diploma in that field but I was more interested in creating internal and external change, than a wall full of credentials.

While this journey of discovery was massively exciting, there was something missing. I felt as if I was finding individual pieces to the puzzle of life. I met people with wonderful relationships who had one piece of the puzzle. I mixed with great business leaders who had a different piece of the puzzle and knew the secrets of finance and power. But the complete picture of the puzzle continued to elude me.

What I was looking for was to feel integrated internally and externally. Internally I wanted to feel whole, strong, loving, motivated and balanced. Externally I wanted what I now call "holistic success". While I had a successful career, it never felt like me. I felt as if I was living someone else's dream. I wanted a career that I truly loved, a great relationship and family, supportive friends and a rich spiritual life. I wanted holistic success.

> *"There is only one success — to be able to spend your life in your own way."*
>
> CHRISTOPHER MORLEY

What I would like to share with you in these pages is a revelation that has turned not only my life around, but the lives of thousands of people I have worked with in my seminars over the last 12 years.

I have encountered many people who have been to the "shopping mall" of self improvement and still not found a way to achieve holistic success. I can see them now in my mind. When I first met Daniel he had a seven figure yearly income and not a true friend in the world. Daniel had mastered the business world but lacked a spiritual centre and felt lonely. He had tried everything to gain some peace of mind.

Dianne, on the other hand, had a very deep spiritual nature but was always on the brink of poverty and could never seem to attract the right partner for a fulfiling relationship.

Everyone described Steve as "lovely" but he never exuded any personal power. He always said that he felt as if he was in the wrong career and struggled with money. He felt constantly buffeted by the changing tides of life.

Then there was Sharon who had fantastic health but complained about her marriage feeling flat. Ray, on the other hand, had a wonderful relationship and family but could never seem to stick to a sensible diet.

It seemed to me as I looked around that there were very few people who had it all; very few who seemed to have holistic success — abundance in their spiritual and emotional worlds and in their relationships, careers and families. As I began to dig deeper I found that very few people were really integrated. It was as if some people had certain qualities that allowed them to attract money and others had qualities that produced spiritual contentment or a fantastic relationship. Very few people seemed to have the lot. Real holistic success.

I wanted the lot. My personal quest began: to find a way to feel whole and integrated internally and to achieve holistic success.

I now look back on my marriage break up as a great blessing. It forced me to look at myself with brutal honesty and to see certain behavioural patterns that I had not seen previously. In fact it would be more honest to say that I began to see things in myself that I had been unwilling to see before.

Immediately after the break up, I experienced every emotion including blame, self-recrimination, anger, grief and a feeling of failure. However, behind these feelings was the quiet, certain knowledge that there was some part of my personality make-up that had brought this upon myself. Most people blame the other person when something goes wrong in a relationship, but that way they never learn the lesson of what it is about themselves that has created the situation in the first place. If you don't learn the lesson and change yourself, you run the risk of repeating the same scenario. If you get into a new relationship or life situation without fixing the core issue, you are bound to face another disaster.

It is crucial that you get to the point of the problem so that you can change it. Imagine that you go out and buy a beautiful new stereo system. You assemble the stereo system and plug it into the power point. Unbeknownst to you, the power point is faulty, and as you switch on your new system it dramatically blows up. After getting over your initial shock, you begin to trace the fault. At first you think that the fault lies within the new system, but you explore all the possibilities and eventually discover that the fault is in the power point. You fix the point and when you get your next system it works just fine.

Now, what would you say to someone who bought stereo after stereo, plugging them into the same point and seeing each system ends in disaster? You would probably shake your head in disbelief.

My marriage had blown up, and I was committed to fixing the root of the problem — myself. I really wanted to discover the answer of how I could achieve holistic success. Deep down I knew that there must be some truth, some secret that would give me the success, peace and wholeness I wanted. I knew that if I wanted holistic success then it would have to start with me. The patterns of your success and failure lie within you. Being successful spiritually, materially and in relationships starts with accessing internal aspects of yourself.

THE SEARCH FOR THE SECRET

It was the collapse of my first marriage that gave me an insight into what I call "the code," which opens the way to holistic success.

Several weeks after my wife and I finally separated, I approached a close friend who knew me very well. We sat in his lounge room and I asked him if he would do me a favour.

I said, "I'm going to sit here and shut my mouth and I want you to tell me how I screwed up my marriage." I mentally prepared myself for a long barrage of information. The answer took me by surprise.

My friend gazed at me intently and said, "That's easy, you don't listen."

I felt a bit stunned by the reply. There was a long pause in the conversation as the information slowly filtered its way through my mental defences. I realised it was true. I could often repeat back exactly what was said in a conversation, but I wasn't really there. I was more concerned with where my own thoughts were taking me, often living in the future, trying to be one step ahead of myself rather than being present.

I began to take notice of a friend of mine who was a tremendous listener. He had a particular make-up that seemed to produce those listening skills. I knew I could learn listening skills, but this seemed an ad hoc solution, not a holistic one. I knew from the past that if you learnt a new skill in a controlled way, later down the track that new skill could be forgotten. I was after a more permanent solution. I felt as if a whole new part within me was lying dormant and needed to be developed.

I began to notice that certain people had a particular make-up or patterning that produced certain results in the world. As I dug deeper in my research, I realised that each one of us has an internal code that is made up of very distinct aspects or elements. When these aspects are unknowingly suppressed they show up as a lack of success or fulfilment in the world. Just as every human being has a DNA coding that shapes them physically, you also have another type of code that determines your level of personal balance and your results in the world. When you unlock this code, it allows you to have more internal range and a larger magnitude of talents at your disposal. The more range you have, the more multifaceted you are in the world.

Imagine a machine that is designed to produce arrows. You look at the machine and say, "Machine, I love arrows; arrows are direct, they find their way to the target, but today I want paper flowers. I want to see some beauty."

What does the machine say? Nothing. It just continues making arrows.

If you want paper flowers you have two choices: build a second machine or expand the original machine to be able to build arrows and paper flowers. I like the second option better. If I can have within me more range it is going to affect my results in the world. Some singers master the low range and others master the high range. Then there are the true masters who can sing in any range.

I have met people who have had a series of unsuccessful relationships or financial problems who seek a remedy. The remedy rarely works until some changes takes place inside.

What I am talking about here is *mastery*. Unlocking your code opens the door to personal mastery. To have mastery in your life creates freedom. I know people in businesses who always struggle to find loyal staff. They say to me there's no loyalty in workers anymore. Yet if they were to unlock their code, they would have an abundance of loyalty in their lives.

I have always believed that if it is possible for one person to have success, then everyone can have it. If one person can have a great relationship, spiritual wisdom or financial success, then we can all have it. It's not just luck, it's knowing how to open your inner code.

If you look at people who have holistic success, you will see a striking similarity. Every person I have encountered who has acquired this wide-ranging success has the same characteristics. The personalities are different, but the characteristic attributes are the same. These attributes, I would like to stress, are not achieved through a series of quick fix techniques, rather they are a deep and profound unfolding of that person's own elements. They are authenticity itself.

In this book, you will find the key to this holistic success as well as discovering your true authentic self. I do not offer you a cosmetic solution, but rather a way of affecting lasting change. If you want the external events of your life to really change, you first need to change your inner world.

We have two lives. The first is the life we lead, the second is our ideal life. This second life sits quietly in the wings, waiting until we discover who we truly are. At that moment our authentic, ideal life takes centre stage and we embrace our destiny.

If you hunger to find a career that is your passion and also lucrative; if you seek a relationship that is full of romance, love and feels like home; if you crave to feel at home in your own skin; if you want to develop an experiential, real connection to God or the Divine Force that is all around us, then I welcome you as a fellow traveller on the path.

THE DISCOVERY OF THE FIVE ELEMENTS:

How to find yourself, become successful and attain spiritual peace

"The great seal of truth is simplicity."

SIMON BOEHAAVE

How do you move from *wanting* a life that is blessed and abundant to *having* it?

The answer lies in awakening the five elements that create your ideal destiny. Opening these elements is like unlocking a five part code. Opening one part of the code leads to new abilities and and more of the real you. When you awaken all five elements you become integrated and achieve a state called *the Quintessence.*

The Oxford Dictionary defines quintessence as the "purest and most perfect form or manifestation or embodiment of a quality." A quintet is defined as "a group of five." When you combine the five elements in harmony, you experience the Quintessence and feel a sense of personal wholeness and balance. It is like a five petalled flower that suddenly blooms. When this flower opens you become awake and alive. You start to resonate more with who you are. Unlocking your five elements and achieving the Quintessence is the key to awakening heaven and earth, and living a life that is successful and spiritually centred.

These elements reflect five distinct aspects of who you are. In some people these aspects are active while in others they lie dormant.

The five elements and their corresponding aspects are:

1. EARTH—THE VISIONARY LEADER

2. FIRE—THE ACHIEVER

3. WATER—THE POET

4. AIR—THE SAGE

5. SPIRIT

Let's examine clearly at what these elements look like and how they determine your destiny.

THE FIVE ELEMENTS WITHIN YOU

1. The Visionary Leader: UNLEASHING YOUR POWER AND LIFE'S PURPOSE

Element — EARTH

The Visionary Leader is the part of yourself that knows your *Grand Purpose.* Your Grand Purpose is your compass, your personal mission, where you are meant to be going. When your compass is working correctly it tells you what your unique direction is in the world. It lets you know what is the appropriate career for you.

Allan was once participating in one of my seminars. Everything in his life was going well except for his career. He was charismatic and vibrant until he started to talk about his job.

"Everyday I wake up and it is a huge effort to get to work," he said. "I have to literally drag myself down the stairs and into the car because I absolutely loathe my job. I'm good at it, but I know it isn't me. I feel like I've lost my way. I feel as if I have so much more to give to the world."

When I asked Allan what he loved to do, he talked about his writing. His whole face lit up. That night he read three of his poems. The whole group sat mesmerised at the depth of his talent. Many people were moved to tears. Allan worked on developing his Visionary Leader and he is now on the way to publishing his first book.

Your Visionary Leader provides you with your purpose, your gift to the world. Like the element of earth, your internal Visionary Leader is a grounding influence in your life and gives you a sense of meaning.

When you look at great leaders such as Martin Luther King, Aung San Suu Kyi and Mahatma Gandhi you see human beings with a tremendous vision and a clear direction. Their purpose has been a gift to the world. Countless books have been written about these people, reflecting our incessant desire to somehow capture what these people had or have. The Visionary Leader enables you to rise above the mundane and seek extraordinary fulfilment.

Being a Visionary Leader does not necessarily mean running an empire. It could be as simple as being the leader of your own life. Reflecting the element of earth, Visionary Leaders are rock solid in their own direction. They follow their own cause. They are their own person. More than anything, the Visionary Leader lets you unfurl the sails of your unique destiny.

The Visionary Leader also provides a balanced, overall plan for your life. If you get too focused on just one area of your life at the expense of other important areas, it addresses the balance.

HOW THE VISIONARY LEADER HELPS YOU ATTAIN HOLISTIC SUCCESS

When you awaken the Visionary Leader, you know who you are and what you stand for. This knowledge affects not only your inner world but ripples out to every area of your life.

CALLE CERNíCALO, LA OLIVA
LAS PALMAS, SPAIN

Sunday, 25 Dec, 2022 at 8:10 AM

Apple iPhone 13 | ISO 50 | 26 mm | 0 ev | f1.6 | 1/544 s |

FP241550310506

INNER LIFE

You feel centred and poised. You know your unique path, and this knowledge gives you a grounded feeling, reflecting the element of Earth.

RELATIONSHIP

When you know who you are and what you stand for, you draw the appropriate person into your life. When you *really* know yourself, you don't fall into the "co-dependent" trap. Staying strong in your own centre, you can love your partner without losing your own identity.

FAMILY LIFE

Have you ever seen a family where the children rule the parents? Children need healthy, loving direction without being dominated. I have worked with a lot of teenagers, quite a few of whom felt they had to be the parent to their own parents. They felt as if they had to grow up before their time. Children that receive loving direction feel more secure.

CAREER

The Visionary Leader leads you to the career or pursuit that is most in alignment with yourself. Your work takes on a sense of meaning.

SOCIAL LIFE

When the Visionary Leader awakens, you no longer become "all things to all people." You attract people that are on your wavelength. These relationships become a tremendous source of strength and nourishment, and support your unique evolutionary path.

MATERIAL WORLD

Have you ever been into someone's house and thought "This house completely reflects this persons personality?" It is called congruence when someone lives in a house and wears a style of clothing that reflects who they really are. Someone who has embraced this element is not easily led into the latest fashion to please others but rather develops their own unique style. The Visionary Leader aligns your inner world with your external surroundings.

SPIRITUAL LIFE

The Visionary Leader helps you choose a spiritual path that is in alignment with who you are. Often people who become involved in cults are out of touch with their Visionary Leader. Lacking their own sense of leadership, they hand over the reins of their destiny to the group leader. The Visionary Leader allows you to learn from others without losing your own sense of power.

2. THE ACHIEVER:
FANNING THE FIRE OF SUCCESS

Element—FIRE

The Achiever is the part of you that goes for the goal, your outcome. A friend of mine who competes in sport at a very high level often tells me right before an event that he's "on fire". Like fire, Achievers burn their way to their goal. They see what they want and they go for it.

When I first met Jade she was in telemarketing. It was obvious that she nursed a fierce, determined will and strong desire to make it to the top. She was very self-competitive, always challenging herself to do more. When she locked onto a target she was like a long distance runner who comes around the final corner and sees the finishing line. Every resource is channelled into crossing that line. After becoming the top person in her office and eventually sales manager, Jade set further goals eventually leading to her appointment as the editor of one of the largest magazines in Europe.

With persistence and drive there is almost no height too great for an Achiever to scale. They love to challenge themselves and are often fiercely competitive.

Sometimes, without the Visionary Leader, they can become successful even when they feel as if they are in the wrong profession, not on the right track. Ideally the Achiever works for the Visionary Leader. Your Visionary Leader comes up with the purpose and then the Achiever makes it happen. The Visionary Leader becomes inspired by the lofty vision of scaling Everest. The Achiever gets you to the top. It takes the dream and makes it a reality.

HOW THE ACHIEVER HELPS YOU ATTAIN HOLISTIC SUCCESS

When you awaken the Achiever, not only does it affect your inner world, but it ripples out to the following areas:

INNER LIFE

Internally you feel awake, alive and alert. You develop drive and persistence. The Achiever is the one that keeps you on that diet or the much needed exercise program.

RELATIONSHIP

The Achiever gives you the strength to ride out the rough spots in a relationship and stay committed to your partner.

FAMILY LIFE

The Achiever gives you the energy and drive that is important in a family. Every family needs someone who is in the driver's seat and who is taking the family to their shared goals. The Achiever provides the commitment that is so important in holding everyone together.

CAREER

The Achiever takes your dream and makes it happen. It gives you the discipline to overcome obstacles and get to your goal.

SOCIAL LIFE

People feel you can be counted on when you have the strength of the Achiever. It creates relationships with substance.

MATERIAL WORLD

The Achiever gives you the drive to pursue your material goals and achieve them.

SPIRITUAL LIFE

Without the Achiever you don't travel very far on the Spiritual path. It gives you the discipline to engage in spiritual practice. I know of no more challenging work than stilling the mind through practices like meditation. The Achiever gives you the drive to grow and evolve.

3. THE POET:
THE ANSWER TO JOY, LOVE AND AMAZING RELATIONSHIPS

Element—WATER

No two elements are as opposite to each other as the Poet and the Achiever, just as water and fire are opposites. Like the nurturing qualities of water, the Poet nurtures you and your loved ones. A plant without water eventually shrivels and dies.

The Poet is all about being in the moment. It is spontaneity, joy, love and innocence. It is the realm of guilelessness. If you would like to see the Poet in action, follow the movements of a small child. If you could condense the nature of the Poet in one word, it would be Heart. Whereas the Achiever is constantly going for a goal and is in a state of doing, the Poet is simply being in the moment. If you've ever been in love then you know the Poet.

Deborah is a classic Poet. Everyone in our local area says that Deborah brings laughter and sunshine wherever she goes. At work she is always trying to bring people together and create harmony. She seems to have a dozen things going at any given time, from assisting at the local school to baking cookies for a friend that needs cheering up. When you are with her, you genuinely feel that she cares about you and has time for you. Children love her too because she is still a kid at heart and always has time to play with them. Her favourite hobbies are walking on the beach at sunset and painting. Deborah is a true poet. Poets love life, people and expressing their creativity.

The Poet is crucial as it brings life, love, joy and hope to your world. It is there all the time in every sunrise and rising moon. Without the Poet you cannot truly experience the beauty of people and the world.

HOW THE POET HELPS YOU ATTAIN HOLISTIC SUCCESS

INNER LIFE

The Poet gives you a sense of beauty, love and joy. Without it, life is like dry toast.

RELATIONSHIP

The Poet provides love and romance in your relationship. It provides the spark that keeps the flame alive.

FAMILY LIFE

Love, harmony and understanding provide the glue that binds a family together. When you embrace the Poet, people feel cared about and nourished.

CAREER

Poets are the people who bring harmony to the team. Your own Poet also gives you the balance that saves you from burning out as the Achiever drives you to your goals.

SOCIAL LIFE

The Poet gives your relationships with your friends a greater level of intimacy. You feel as if you can trust people and let them in. Your friends feel that you have an empathic ear, and feel nourished by your company.

MATERIAL WORLD

The Poet brings beauty to your surroundings. People who have developed their Poet bring a nurturing feeling to their external environment. They know how to spend money on looking after themselves.

SPIRITUAL LIFE

Any spiritual path without a heart isn't worth pursuing. Most of the world religions and great spiritual philosophies have at their core, the saying, "God is Love".

4. THE SAGE: OPENING THE DOOR TO INNER PERCEPTION AND WISDOM

Element—AIR

People who are imbued with the Sage have tremendous wisdom. They have the ability to see people and situations as they really are. Their primary ally is intuition. In indigenous tribes they are commonly referred to by outsiders as shamans, medicine men or medicine women.

Like the element of air that is unconstrained, the Sage isn't bound by physical senses.

A Jewish friend of mine told me the story of how his father emigrated from Europe to Australia in the 1930s. His father was sixteen years of age when he began to feel a sense of impending doom. He was assured by almost everyone that there was no danger, yet still this feeling gnawed within. Against all logic, and motivated by this intuition, he finally decided to leave his homeland to travel to the other side of the world. It took a lot of courage as he boarded the train, saying his last farewells to his family. He was leaving a familiar place and journeying into the unknown. As he waved goodbye to his parents, he had no idea that it would be the last time he would ever see them.

They were caught up in the horror of the holocaust. His intuition had saved him from a similar fate.

As he grew up, all his friends used to refer to him as "the wise old professor." People who are imbued with the Sage often have this air about them. It is this wisdom which gives them an edge in this world. Often they are able to sense opportunities others miss.

Sages are like air — they can be hard to grasp hold of — but this quality allows them to move into places beyond the physical. If you have ever had the experience of the telephone ringing and *knowing* who it was before you picked it up, you have been in touch with your own Sage. If you have ever walked into old churches or buildings and sensed a certain atmosphere that is not present outside, you have felt your Sage. It may not seem rational, yet you and others feel it.

In Western cultures this particular element is often considered strange and illogical. The irony is that most people I know who have achieved great success attribute much of it to "a gut feeling." I know a very successful Wall Street businessman whose favourite quote is "got a hunch, bet a bunch!"

HOW THE SAGE HELPS YOU ATTAIN HOLISTIC SUCCESS

INNER LIFE

The Sage gives you a feeling of wisdom and depth. It gives you a multi-dimensional approach to the world and enhances your lateral thinking.

RELATIONSHIP

The Sage gives you the ability to say the right thing at the right time. Being able to tune in to your partner in this way enables you to perceive small problems in the relationship before they grow into big problems.

FAMILY LIFE

It is important to be able to sense when someone needs help. The Sage knows when to offer support to family members and when to give them space so that they can make their own choices and decisions.

CAREER

Have you ever been with someone in a meeting who chimes in with the exact information that's needed at a given moment? The Sage allows you to sense opportunities and avoid pitfalls.

SOCIAL LIFE

The Sage gives you the wisdom and intuition to choose friends that are loving and supportive. Having a friend that has the wisdom of the Sage is a tremendous asset.

MATERIAL WORLD

More fortunes are lost by not following your intuition than for any other reason, and countless successful ventures have begun from an intuitive hunch. The Sage gives you the ability to be in the right place at the right time. I have spoken with many great investors who attribute their success to combining good research with intuitive timing. Rather than follow the crowd, they listen to their own inner wisdom.

SPIRITUAL LIFE

Wisdom gives you the ability to clearly identify a spiritual practice that works. The Sage enables you to discern between a fad and something that has substance, integrity and lasting effect.

5. SPIRIT:

AWAKENING TO YOUR SPIRITUAL POTENTIAL

The fifth element is your own spirit, or soul; your eternal, animating principle. Your spirit is something beyond your senses, your body and your mind. It lives on after your physical body ends. As it is outside the realm of the physical, it has no elemental structure.

Spirit is not to be confused with the fiery spirit of the Achiever. I am often asked what does Spirit feel like? When there isn't a single thought in your mind, when your emotions are still and when all you feel is a sense of *beingness*, you are in touch with your Spirit. To be in contact with your own Spirit is not a process of doing, it is a process of undoing. It is about taking the filters away from the light that emanates from within you and letting it shine. Embracing your spirit is not a new philosophy, rather it is an experience that enhances your particular religion or philosophy.

We were secluded in a big open house in Colorado surrounded by a dense green forest on all sides. It was midwinter and the snow was deep on the ground. We had taken a group to see a Native American elder by the name of Richard who had devoted his whole life to furthering his spiritual quest.

As Richard stood to speak, what was most obvious to the group was his deep, quiet presence. Physically he was very tall and large in a raw-boned way, but that was not what was so arresting about him. It was his eyes, truly windows to the soul. Those eyes were powerful and penetrating, yet free of judgement. You got the feeling he was in touch with his own Spirit, as though he was living in an elevated sphere.

One of the members of our group, David, asked Richard about a recurring problem he had been experiencing for most of his life. For as long as he could remember, he was plagued by deep feelings of inadequacy and self doubt. He had tried many different things to combat these feelings. He was extremely successful in his career and in the top one percent of income earners in his country. To many of his colleagues at work he seemed self-assured but he knew a lot of it was just an act.

Richard quietly listened as David spoke, his head cocked slightly to one side. Then when he had finished talking about his dilemma, Richard looked right into his eyes and precipitated what was one of the biggest turning points in this man's life. As he looked into his eyes he simply said, "You're okay."

In that one moment something deep within awakened. David had an experience of his Spirit. He felt a deep peace and certainty flood through him. One soul looked to another soul and transmitted the eternal truth, that beyond the ever-changing personality, we are, and always will be, okay.

Years later, David still talks about that powerful moment. For the first time he could remember, he profoundly *knew* he was okay, and the realisation has never left him.

Without accessing this most priceless aspect of yourself, you are confined to success only in the material world. It is fabulous to achieve great distinction, honour and wealth, but it is your Spirit that keeps it all in perspective. What you do in the world may be important, vital to others, yet still it is a game that one day must end. Although the game may end, you don't. Who you really are, your being, your spirit, continues.

There is a small village in Afghanistan that was once called Ghazni. While it is almost unknown today, one thousand years ago it was regarded as the richest city in Asia. This vast wealth was due to its monarch, King Mahmud, who invaded India seventeen times, stripping that country of its riches to fill his own treasury. On his deathbed he asked his courtiers to carry him on a palanquin through his numerous treasure rooms. On seeing this vast display he was filled with remorse, not only for the countless people who had suffered at his hands but the realisation that none of his accumulated riches were going with him into the life beyond. He requested that at his funeral, his hands be placed outside the casket with his palms upturned, to signify he was leaving this world with nothing.

HOW SPIRIT HELPS YOU ATTAIN HOLISTIC SUCCESS

Being in touch with your Spirit gives you a presence and a sense of peace that filters into every area of your life. It allows you to feel centred and calmer in your relationships and in the world. It also allows you to maintain your responsibilities but to not get so caught up in the day to day world that you lose perspective of just how small your part is in the great game of life. This attitude creates more peace in your life which actually makes you more effective in the world. Rather than worrying about unimportant things, your peace of mind let's you focus on the tasks that really matter.

When I think of all the great rulers who have come and gone, and look at the countless stars in the heavens, it puts everything in perspective. Did you know that there are more stars in the universe than there are grains of sand in all the deserts and beaches of the world? Think about that for a moment. How many countless grains are in one handful of sand? When I tend to get caught up in some "crucial" task it reminds me that although each of our lives are important to the whole network of the universe, ultimately we are tiny strands in that incredibly vast web.

ATTAINING AN EXTRAORDINARY LIFE:

Embracing the five elements

We all have the five elements within us. We are the Sage, the Achiever, the Visionary Leader and the Poet, all wrapped around a timeless, eternal being known as our Spirit. We all possess the inherent tendencies of every element. We don't have to "invent" these elements within us because they are already there, we merely have to develop them.

Before I move on to an in-depth analysis of each element and how you can use it to create a life of your dreams, I will show you some practical examples of how the elements work together to achieve extraordinary success.

Imagine you had a business or a project that you wanted to get off the ground. Your Visionary Leader would come up with the idea, the inspiration and the vision. The Achiever would make sure the vision was activated and completed. The Poet would ensure that you had fun and inspired people's love and warmth to work with you. The Sage would be looking out for pitfalls and correct timing, and your Spirit would keep the whole project in perspective.

When these five elements are integrated, they create success in every area of your life. As a parent, for example, you would be a great leader of the family, but also have the energy of the Achiever and the playfulness of the Poet. With the wisdom of the Sage you would be able to provide counsel and help steer people in the right direction.

I once worked as a consultant for a company whose people were primarily Poets. Everyone in the company said it was one of the warmest and most caring environments they had ever worked in, yet the common complaint was that very little was achieved. People talked about change and financial progress but not much ever happened. Like all Poets, they loved the process itself, rather than aiming to achieve the goal. On the other hand, I have also worked with companies who are full of Achievers, where the common complaint is about a lack of warmth and caring. You need both elements to be activated, in fact all of them, for holistic success.

People who are inspirational knowingly or unknowingly combine all five elements into their life and projects.

Candy Lightner inspired countless people through her personal tragedy. Her daughter was killed in a senseless car accident by a driver under the influence of alcohol. Her vision that more awareness was needed about the repercussions of drink-driving (the Visionary Leader) and compassion for others who had suffered similar tragedies (the Poet) led her to start M.A.D.D. — Mothers Against Drunk Driving. She felt that people were ready to embrace her message (the Sage). Using her energy and passion (the Achiever), Candy's message, and the organisation, spread like wildfire across the United States.

The Quintessence can also happen on a simple but equally profound level, as I witnessed first hand with Mike. It was the first night of one of my seminars and into the room came one of the saddest and most "stuck" people I had ever seen. All I felt was empathy. Physically, Mike looked as dense and inflexible as a brick with legs. He was a man exhibiting both agony and defeat. He was old before his time. His wife had sent him to the seminar desperately hoping that a miracle might occur.

Someone once said that the difference between a rut and a grave is just a few feet, and in Mike's case this was just about true. He later confided to me that he used to go to bed every night hoping he wouldn't wake up in the morning.

Mike's Visionary Leader was active in his business and family, but his Poet was buried so deep that laughter, spontaneity and joy were long gone. The Sage, in his opinion, was something to be greeted with scepticism. All that stuff about there being more to the world than what you could see and touch was for the story books. As for any real spiritual connection, there was none. What Mike did have though was an Achiever, a fierce and determined will.

Through the application and perseverance of many of the principles you will encounter in this book, Mike is now one of the most changed and transformed people I have encountered. His Visionary Leader has opened and he has become an inspiration to his local community where he helps those in need. The Poet can be seen by the smile on his face and the loving twinkle in his eyes. He has a natural Sage-like wisdom which is of enormous benefit to those he counsels, and a deep spiritual awareness which gives him great depth. He looks 10 years younger today than he did all those years ago. In fact the old Mike no longer exists. The authentic person has emerged.

Mike has arrived at his own Quintessence. A whole person. Gaining the Quintessence naturally produced holistic success — a life that is balanced, successful and integrated. He is a person who is comfortable in himself, his marriage and family. He has a network of loving and supportive friends, a material life that he is proud of, and a spiritual life that is real. By real, I mean he exudes a feeling that he is a part of all things and is connected to the Divine Force.

THE FIVE ELEMENTS: THE BASIS OF MYTHS AND LEGENDS

Many of our old myths reflect the human quest to awaken the five elements. The stories that have lasted through the centuries reflect humanity's subconscious desire to understand and awaken all five elements. Quite often the characters depict who we are or who we would wish to become.

Scores of books and movies have been made about King Arthur

and Camelot. Camelot, Arthur's castle, is symbolic of the Quintessence. A time of perfection and a place of power and grace. Everything came together; the land was blessed and people prospered.

Let me take you back in time. There was a period of great unrest thirteen hundred years ago when Britain was ruled by many kings. There was no unifying principle in the land and people felt unsafe. Into this arena rode a young king by the name of Arthur. His vision was to unite all of Britain under one rule so that the land would be blessed and everyone would prosper. Arthur's strongest elements were his Visionary Leader and his Achiever. He had the ability to make his vision happen.

Let's look a little more closely at what he was lacking. He was not a fully developed Poet. Of course, where there is a vacuum something must fill it. Onto the stage came Guinevere and Lancelot. These star-crossed lovers with their impossible love fulfiled the role of the Poet.

Arthur's biggest failing was his inability to see betrayal in those around him. He was completely lacking in his own Sage. Who fulfiled this role? Merlin — the seer who could see into the deepest recesses of people's hearts and minds. Unfortunately, because he was *only* developed in the element of the Sage, Merlin led a life of seclusion. He was unable to develop any real intimate and lasting relationships primarily because of his undeveloped Poet. Many a modern day Sage is confined to the same fate if they do not develop their other elements.

Now the remarkable thing about this cast of characters was that they were linked by a common thread. The knights of the round table were involved in a sacred quest to find the grail — the Spirit. In spite of all the conquests, defeats, joys and sorrows, the quest for the grail elevated these seekers onto a more noble, spiritual plane. It created a higher purpose. As in real life, this quest for the Grail proved to be the simplest yet the most difficult task of all. To truly discover your own spirit, your real self, is the simplest thing to define and yet the most difficult to achieve.

"Star Wars" is another example of a story that has endured across generations. What is it that turned the original "Star Wars" movie into part of our culture? Sure it was entertaining, but one reason it was re-released at the cinema twenty years after it was first screened is that its cast of characters contained all of the five elements.

Han Solo was the Achiever, someone who believed in himself, was practical and was outcome driven. Obe Wan Kanobe had the wisdom, depth and perception of the Sage. The Rebel Alliance was driven by the Visionary Leader on the quest for freedom. Throughout the movie the essence of the Poet, the desire to connect with the world and others, was played out with romance, love and hope. Underlying all of this was the Spirit, which was symbolised by The Force. The Force was the quest to go beyond the mundane and ordinary, and seek out the true nature of ourselves.

HOW THE ELEMENTS WORK IN THE REAL WORLD

The following diagram represents a wheel. For a wheel to travel smoothly over the ground it needs to be a complete circle. When all five elements come together the circle is complete, creating a smooth ride through the journey of your life. The centre or hub of the wheel is your Spirit. When this is awakened it illuminates your entire life. The other elements that make up the wheel make your life fulfiling and successful.

When you achieve the Quintessence, this is what your wheel looks like:

Now let's look at what your wheel would look like with one of the elements missing.

If you were undeveloped in the element of the Poet, you would have difficulties relating to people. Others might perceive you as abrasive or distant. You might respond with caution and a lack of trust. It would be difficult for the wheel to turn over the missing piece. You would be in store for a bumpy ride.

Take another piece out of the wheel and the problem would be compounded. If you lacked both the Poet and the Achiever, your ride would be even more uncomfortable than someone who is undeveloped in just the Poet aspect. You would probably find your relationships and career fizzling out after a short while, and you might experience a lack of enthusiasm and zing in your life.

If your elemental make-up matched the following diagram, you would feel a lack of personal balance.

You can imagine if we took another element out of the picture how that would complicate matters even further. The wheel of life would have great difficulty in turning at all!

OPPOSITES ATTRACT

I often say, in regard to relationships, that you marry or enter into a relationship with what you need to learn. Opposites attract to learn from each other and quite often awaken each other's elements.

Two friends of mine who were in a relationship lived out the classic Poet versus Achiever battle.

The Poet was constantly telling the Achiever, "Why don't you relax, chill out. All this driven focus you have is keeping you out of the flow."

The Achiever was constantly telling the Poet, "You need to be more motivated and committed. You need to get things done."

They were both partially right. I say "partially" right because you don't have to trash an already strong suit to have another aspect. I have seen many people who have read personal development or self-help books make this mistake. It goes something like this: "Boy this book is right, I'm way too pushy, I need to be more cruisey, less controlled — yeah that's it. I'll reinvent a new way of acting and being."

This is an inauthentic response. It is acting rather than coming from your core authentic self. It is just another way of controlling yourself. Authenticity is opening and awakening not controlling. That is why I have never liked the term "reinventing yourself" because it smacks of strategy and control. If you already are a strong Achiever, that's fine. That's what has got you to where you are now. Your Achiever is a friend. Keep that friend with you while you nurture others. It will actually help you develop the other elements.

Many people often have one or two aspects that are developed and yet never work on their dormant elements. This is like a dancer who only works on her best moves but never achieves fulfilment and balance because other aspects of her routine remain untouched.

Imagine the absurdity of a body builder with one massive right arm and an undeveloped left arm. Every day the body builder goes to the gym and works out his strong arm. He does this because it is his favourite arm and besides, he's good at it. Sounds ridiculous, and yet this is exactly what happens to many people. They develop their favourite element, which produces lopsided results.

Joan is a very strong Achiever. She works extremely hard for a large corporation. She gets great satisfaction out of her job, although often feels burned out. Her friends admire her dedication but often feel that there's not much time for them. Like most singular Achievers her focus is very narrow and she only has time for a few extraneous things in her life. If you can get past Joan's strong exterior, she would probably tell you that she often feels lonely, and that all that really interests her is work and perhaps one or two hobbies. Her relationship is becoming ever more distant. She often wonders where all the love has gone.

When she does get a quiet moment to herself, Joan is sure that there has to be more to life than working her way to the top. She senses that there must be some greater meaning to her existence, but somehow it eludes her. She is on the treadmill and can't seem to find the stop button. Even if she did manage to stop, she is terrified that she might just miss her opportunity to get to the top.

On the other hand, Thomas describes himself as a spiritual person. Nothing has ever really worked for him in the world, so he has convinced himself that he really is above it all and doesn't need to succeed like those "poor rats on the revolving wheel." He loves to discuss matters of deep philosophical importance, yet when it comes to handling the basic necessities of life, Thomas really struggles. Women at first love Thomas's depth but pretty soon tire of his lack of passion. Deep down he often feels insecure about his lack of achievement.

Thomas is really a bit of an escapist. This is not true spirituality. As you will discover, truly spiritual people often do the very thing that they are afraid of, because they know that by doing this, their spirituality will continue to evolve. By avoiding experiences that can help you grow, you inhibit your spiritual growth.

Thomas has tried to shortcut the first four elements and go straight for the fifth element. This doesn't work. Just as a rocket-ship needs a platform before it can be launched into the heavens, so too do you need the platform of the Visionary Leader, the Achiever, the Poet, and the Sage in order to contact your Spirit. One of my favourite sayings is "feet on the ground, head in the stars". The first four elements keep your feet on the ground while you aim for the stars on your spiritual quest.

WHO HAS THE QUINTESSENCE?

Before we go on to look at each element in detail, let's look at three extraordinary people and examine why they are extraordinary: The Dalai Lama; Aung San Suu Kyi, winner of the Nobel peace prize; and Nelson Mandela. All of them are Visionary Leaders with a huge vision of freedom. They all possess the child like quality of the Poet and a deep love for humanity. How else could Nelson Mandela have endured 27 years of incarceration and be so genuinely forgiving?

Aung San Suu Kyi was placed under house arrest for six years in Burma, even though the political party she led had won a landslide victory in democratic elections. She has refused to hate her enemies despite the physical and emotional trauma she has suffered. She has remained steadfast to her purpose (the Achiever) while emanating the loving presence of the Poet.

The Dalai Lama, a quiet, loving Poet, tirelessly works for the welfare of his people (the Visionary Leader and Achiever). Through the wisdom of the Sage he has turned his own exile into a situation that has gained his cause a sympathetic hearing around the world. He has extended his role as the leader of Tibet into being a world-renowned spiritual teacher.

These three great people are driven by the Achiever to pursue their goals and outcomes. Once they start something, they don't stop until it is finished. At the same time they have a Sage-like quality that gives them great wisdom and timing. They have used their predicaments to skillfully harness world opinion against their oppressors. A classic Sage manoeuvre.

All three of these leaders, have a sense of spirituality that gives them a deep, peaceful presence. Their lives are not only externally successful but they emanate internal success and inner fulfilment.

They embody the balance between success in the physical world and spiritual world — "feet on the ground, head in the stars".

The alignment of the Five Elements creates a sense of completeness, a sense of balance, joy and happiness. It creates The Quintessence.

BUTTERFLY PERFUME

Have you noticed how some people seem to have an easier road in life than others? Attaining success is a bit like catching a butterfly. You can chase the butterfly, running and struggling to snare the insect. Alternatively, you can wait until the butterfly floats in your direction before you pounce. This second option is a lot easier. When you embrace the Quintessence, it is like wearing butterfly perfume. You naturally attract what you want in life. That is why it is crucial to develop your five elements, not only for success in your outer world but peace and wholeness in your inner world.

The following chapters look at each element in detail. They will guide you as you discover your primary element, and as you work out which elements you need to develop in order to achieve happiness and a fulfiling life. The keys to awakening the life of your dreams lie ahead.

PART TWO

THE FIVE ELEMENTS

PART TWO

THE VISIONARY LEADER

"Some men see things as they are and say why? I dream of things that never were and say why not?"

GEORGE BERNARD SHAW

FROM A DREAM TO DESTINY

I always thought I would be the last person who would find their purpose in the world. Although I knew that the key to life was the pursuit of personal evolution, there didn't seem to be any jobs that I was really passionate about. Most of my friends leaving school were making career choices based on logic rather than passion. Everyone seemed to be doing a remarkable job of hiding their confusion from themselves and others–a bunch of bright young faces heading down the road of life towards an unknown destination. Many seemed to rush ahead as fast as they could, hoping they'd land in the right place. Sadly though, as the years rolled by, quite a few felt as though they had lost who they were on the way to getting there.

I saved some money and, with a surfboard under one arm, headed off in search of adventure. Adventure I found in abundance. I worked as a farm hand on a remote station in north west Australia. With a box of completely unfamiliar tools, I talked my way onto an oil refinery in South Africa. I met some amazing characters in Madagascar but still came no closer to discovering my purpose in life.

I finally landed in my own business, marketing large Real Estate projects. I was handling multimillion dollar contracts—Italian clothes,

German cars, success. I was mixing with multimillionaires who played life hard, fast and with pot loads of money. I was respected in the industry as someone who could take an extremely difficult project and make it fly.

My business became a vehicle where I could challenge myself and others to grow and evolve. I seemed to attract people who were spiritually deep but had never been successful in the world. Traditional staff meetings were abolished and replaced with training sessions where I implemented all my years of research into peak human potential. We were one of the most successful firms in our field. The catchcry of other firms was "perform, sell, sell sell". While we were saying– "grow, grow, grow". We had an entire team of people who meditated.

I changed the definition of a successful business from an entity that makes money, to a vehicle that allows people to transform, grow and change. In fact if you wanted a job in the company your current skill level was largely irrelevant. There was only one question you had to answer. "How passionate are you about being all you can be?"

I loved watching the changes in the staff. People would come into the business who had little confidence and suddenly bloom. The company flourished and every salesperson was in the top one percent of producers in the country.

There was only one problem. I felt like a fish out of water. The business I was in didn't feel like me. I believed, deep down, that every one of us has a secret passion, a special gift to offer the world–our own glove. I felt like I was wearing some other person's glove. It was a great glove, however, it still didn't feel like mine.

I would meet old school friends and we would all do the same dance. On the outside were the smiles of success, and on the inside were a whole bunch of kids wondering what had happened? What had happened to all those dreams, hopes and aspirations? Some avoided the answer by continuing down the same road at an even faster pace.

I was hungry to find my own tailor-made glove, my unique dream. I knew I had to leave my business. If I stayed on the same track, the outcome would be predictable. I could see myself in twenty years–

successful, slightly dead and unfulfilled. I wanted my own glove.

I started asking myself the question, "What is my purpose?" I kept asking that question with as much passion as I could muster. I didn't stop asking until I found the answer. Finally, after six months, five words came to me. The answer was very simple and very, very clear: "To empower myself and others." To me these five words had integrity. I had tried the path of just empowering myself through meditation and other disciplines, and that had felt a little self-obsessive, like half the picture. I was also wary of those who were only on a mission to save the world. Their sentiment looked good on the outside, but they seemed lacking in any personal awareness of what may be happening on the inside. My emotional response was, "Save yourself first."

I knew in my gut that I had to leave my business. There were quite a few people who thought I was nuts, walking away from the money, but I felt if I didn't take the risk and commit myself to change, part of me would die.

During the previous three years I had been leading personal growth seminars part-time and I knew that this was what I really wanted to do. So, with the support of my wife, Annie, I jumped ship. We spent six weeks promoting the first seminar of my new career. I felt energised and focussed, completely on track. The seminar was successful and all the participants loved it, even though at the end of the day, we came away with a grand total of $200 profit.

Those first 18 months were very difficult. I now know, looking back, that they were a test. Was I going to stay committed to my vision? We had no money, and I mean *no* money. Many was the day when we literally did not have two bucks for a coffee. Going from a high income to no income was a real shock to the system. I went from a bright red Porsche to a very old, faded blue Datsun. There were days when I felt embarrassed driving down the street. However, there were omens I was on the right track.

In one of my training sessions during this time, a tough, nuggety-built man in his early thirties was sent by his company to take part. He was the full-blown corporate climber and was very sceptical about what I was offering. At the end of the first day he approached me with tears in his eyes. He told me that when we had started talking about kids, he had had an astounding revelation. He realised that he was completely ignoring his son. From that moment on, he decided to forge a bond with his son and let him know that he loved him.

I thought to myself, "If that's all I ever do, help some kid who doesn't even know me, then that's enough." Just in that one moment of decision I witnessed a father alter the entire course of his son's life. I knew that this was what the work was really about—creating the possibility for ourselves and others to choose a more liberating life.

Despite the times of great reward and insight, I still had moments of doubt. One day I buckled. I got a job selling advertising space door-to-door in order to bring in some money. On my first morning on the job, I walked through a small industrial area: tired, worn looking buildings built only for function, clinging to the edge of town. I walked into a concrete cavern that housed a machinist shop. The oil-mottled floor was littered with an array of machines, and the air carried the smell of burnt oil. I stood in the middle of the shop going through my spiel to a very patient business owner, but I knew in my gut I was way off track. I was so grateful when he said no. And with that, my advertising career ended as quickly as it began.

After a year of continuing our seminars with very little money, we came up with a new idea. I had built up a large following in New Zealand when I was teaching seminars part-time, and we decided to market a long-term seminar to our New Zealand graduate base, to be held in Australia. Enrolments started pouring in from people who were willing to fly in from New Zealand. It looked like it was going to be a huge success. We couldn't believe it. This would solve all our problems

THE TURNING POINT

Just as it looked like everything was running as it should be, out of the blue a voice started whispering in my head, an inner impulse. "Go to Colorado." I started to get the strongest, deepest feeling that we had to go to America. It felt as if something incredibly important was waiting for us there. At first my response was, "You've got to be kidding, not now, just when things are starting to happen". But the inner impulse got stronger and stronger. It began to feel clearly wrong to chose to run this particular seminar and not go to Colorado. There was no logic to support this, just a very strong intuition. I had never cancelled an event before, but I felt as if I couldn't teach people to follow their own intuition if I wasn't willing to follow mine. We refunded the money, sold everything we had, and headed to the United States with a feeling that something was waiting for us.

After a few days in Colorado, we found ourselves in Durango, a beautiful town surrounded by snow-capped mountains. Sitting in a coffee shop, we pulled out a map to figure out where we were going for the day. We spotted a little town on an Indian Reservation and both got the strongest feeling to go there. An hour later I was standing in this tiny town in a gift shop. There was a Native American woman behind the counter. On an impulse, I asked her if there was anyone around who conducted Native American ceremonies.

Now at this point, you've got to understand that asking that sort of question was not the "done thing." Genuine Native American Medicine Men are often wary of white outsiders. Anyway, she cocked her head slightly to the side, sized me up, walked over to a cassette box and pulled out a card. "Call this guy."

We called the man and he arranged to meet us in a restaurant. It was one of those places with loads of character: cheap food, scattered booths and tables, a cross between a diner from the fifties and a John Wayne movie set. It was definitely a locals-only hang-out, full of smoke, grizzled cowboys and Native Americans. We started talking to our new friend, asking him if he knew anyone who led sweatlodges. A sweatlodge is a sacred ceremony where rocks are placed in a large fire to heat up. These red hot rocks are then brought into a dome like structure called an inipi or lodge. Physically it's like having a sauna in the dark, although this is a very crude analogy. A well run sweatlodge has a very powerful atmosphere.

At first our contact was amazed at us asking, and then he called out to someone a few tables away. "Hey Uncle, there are two people here who want to do a sweat." His Uncle came over. He was a solid man in his fifties, with two long plaits, a powerful presence and piercing eyes that went right through you. We talked for a while but in the end he remained very non-committal. He politely said his farewells and left. Minutes later he walked back through the door of the restaurant and headed straight up to our table. Looking intently at us, he said, "There's a sweatlodge for you two, tonight at 6 o'clock."

It turned out that "Uncle" was a highly respected medicine man. When he had walked out of the restaurant, the first person he had run into was an old Indian whose land the sweat lodge was on. He had then crossed the street and the next person he had met was the guy who had the firewood. He had felt these meetings too much of an omen to ignore.

That night we were the only white people in an all Indian ceremony. The sweatlodge was the beginning of a whole new journey. Uncle and his relations took us in as family and shared their knowledge with us. It was a truly amazing time. We sat inside the darkened confines of the lodge, the hot rocks glowing in the centre of the circle like giant red hearts. We listened to ancient wisdom and were taught ceremonies that were handed down through families for hundreds of years. I felt honoured and privileged.

We settled in Colorado, living on a secluded, winding country road in the woods, surrounded by pine trees, deer and other forest dwellers. In the quiet of the night we could hear the tinkling of the stream that ran over the river stones at the front of our place. Every day was pure magic. It felt like we could not put a foot wrong. Everywhere we went we met the most remarkable people and teachers. Life was a synchronistic adventure.

On the outside, I was having some amazing experiences, and within myself I began to feel a powerful transformation. It was as if the real me was beginning to emerge. I felt I was becoming authentic in the real sense of the word, more genuine. In comparison, the "old me" felt like a cardboard cut-out. I was feeling alive, wild and centred.

After five months, we returned home significantly changed. It was a full year and half since I had first leapt off the cliff to lead seminars full-time. During that period I had experienced some glorious highs and a lot of inner turmoil. I was a changed person as a result of it all. I had finally arrived at the place where I thought, "Oh, what the hell. If this is the way it has to be, with no money, we'll just keep going with our courses anyway." It is called surrender. Surrender isn't giving up, it is the active state of following divine will rather than personal will. It had taken me eighteen months of wriggling like a fish trying to get off the hook before I surrendered.

Within a month of arriving back home, my courses took off. I believe it was a result of the changes that had taken place within me, as mysterious forces guide our destiny when we take the first committed step. People called out of the blue wanting to promote our seminars. We weren't doing anything differently, but suddenly there was an explosion of energy around my work. For a while there, it seemed as if I had two addresses. One of them was the airport, where I was on my way to some talk or seminar.

The Visionary Leader allowed me to discover who I really was and what I stood for. This process of authenticity unfolded for me in Colorado.

THE VISIONARY LEADER'S BLUEPRINT

The element associated with the Visionary Leader is earth. Think of someone who is grounded, solid as a rock, a tower of strength, and you are thinking of a Visionary Leader. The Visionary Leader is grounded in who they are and what they stand for. They have a strength and solidity that comes from living their unique dream or vision. Their lives are full of meaning because there is a deep recognition that they are here to fulfil a greater purpose. They are their own person, and the knowledge of what they are here to do, gives them great clarity and a sense of magnetism.

Visionary Leaders embark on a courageous journey to be themselves and embrace their personal vision. They are like captains on a ship that sail out into the ocean seeking new horizons. Whether these ships carry a crew of a hundred or a solo sailor, there is only one captain on each ship. These captains, or Visionary Leaders, have realised that whether they have hundreds of followers or work on their own, it is their unique individual star they must navigate towards. They have left the safety of the shoreline and the mass of people who take security in fitting in with the status quo. These courageous captains often feel misunderstood or lonely, for when they look out into the world, they cannot find many of their own kind.

Like all captains on all ships, eventually they have to return to port. Those who are wise, seek out other captains to share travel tales and inspiration before heading back out to sea. Those that are less wise avoid each other or compete amongst themselves. They feel more secure surrounded by their unquestioning followers.

Visionary Leaders who are truly in their power feel refreshed and renewed when they are in the company of their own kind. Often they are people who have taken on heavy responsibilities. Sometimes, because of the uniqueness of their individual vision, they cannot remain on someone else's 'boat' or project for very long. If you find someone whose vision is very similar to your own, a tremendous alliance can be made. This can be true in any arena, whether it be in business or in your personal life.

In a relationship, the alliance of two people sharing a similar vision produces two strong individuals who can stand in their own power and not have to compete with each other. This lays the foundation for a great relationship and eliminates co-dependency, where one or both of the individuals give in to the will of the other.

When you awaken your Visionary Leader, you know who you are and what you stand for. You know what your purpose is in life, and you are deeply motivated to fulfil this purpose and maximise your potential. You become someone who is magnetic. This magnetism emanates from your clear direction of what your life is about.

THE THREE STEPS TO DISCOVERING YOUR LIFE'S PURPOSE

The first great quality of the Visionary Leader is Purpose

STEP 1: UNDERSTANDING YOUR GRAND PURPOSE

The first step in understanding and developing your Visionary Leader is discovering the broad purpose of your life. The discovery of your purpose is the foundation to becoming motivated beyond your dreams. When you find your life's purpose, you have achieved the first great quality of the Visionary Leader.

When you look at nature, you can see purpose in everything. To the casual observer it may look as if trees and plants do no more than grow, exist and die. However, a closer look reveals that they provide habitats for countless animals, birds and insects, and they provide oxygen and food for the planet. Without them, we could not survive. The trees and plant life make an overall contribution to the planet. They have a purpose.

Without purpose human beings become demoralised. Stalin found that the quickest way to demoralise political prisoners in the Gulags was to make them dig holes and then fill them in again. Over time, the prisoners lost their motivation to resist and fight, and became very easy to guard.

To be in a career, relationship or any other situation which has no perceived purpose is also slowly demoralising. People who are in these situations begin to lose their motivation. When you find your purpose, you find your ideal occupation and lifestyle, and you automatically feel motivated.

The word "motivation" comes from the word "motive." Think of one of those old detective movies, where the detective arrives at the scene of the crime wearing a trench coat and dark hat. As he walks into the room, a weary policeman looks up from the prostrate victim and says, "Well chief, it's *moider* of da foist degree." The detective looks flatly back and replies, "Let's establish a motive." Detectives know that human beings only do something for a reason, a purpose.

If you know somebody who resembles the corpse at the crime scene by exhibiting near zero motivation it is because they don't have a reason or motive to get going with their life.

Let me give you an example. You're staying in a little cottage tucked away in the wilderness. You have been working extremely hard on a big project and are exhausted. You really need this time away to rejuvenate. You decide that exploring the peaceful woodland that begins down near the back fence is the perfect tonic. Grabbing your backpack and a few supplies, you head out the door and over the fence. Entering the woodland there is an incredible sense of peace. Hardly a leaf is stirring on this warm sunny morning. Birds flutter between trees. You can smell the new growth of spring.

As you head into the centre of the woods you hear the sound of running water. You climb down a steep slope and there in front of you is a beautiful crystal clear stream. The setting is so breath-taking that a quiet "wow" escapes your lips in appreciation of this little sanctuary. "I'll just sit here for a while," you think to yourself, "and forget all about the world."

Feeling lethargic, you take off your backpack and settle down in the crook of a tree to enjoy the view. As you exhale a large breath of air in complete relaxation, you hear a growling noise behind you. You quietly turn to see a huge menacing bear advancing towards you. There is a small moment of shock and then only one thought enters your mind. *Survival.* Your entire purpose at that moment of your life is to *live*. As you sprint away you find an energy inside you that you never dreamed you had. You speedily scramble up the steep slope with ease. The last sound you hear is the bear devouring the food in your backpack.

Now, what happened here? From where did you find that tremendous energy? From the all-consuming and crystal clear motivation to survive. There are stories of mothers lifting massive weights off their trapped babies, weights that in a normal situation they would be unable to lift. How is this possible? It is because in that precise moment of time they find a purpose inside themselves that motivates them beyond their wildest imagination.

I was once asked if I was a motivator. "No", I replied. "I get people in touch with their own motives so that they can motivate themselves." I have watched many people return from a classic motivation speech, energised and raring to go, only to fall flat a few days later. Why? Because these pep talks are often a quick fix solution. What is the point of motivating someone who deep down isn't really passionate about what they are doing?

The key to being motivated is to find your purpose. When you find your purpose, you know your direction. Most people who seem to wander through their lives aimlessly aren't lazy, they just don't know where they are going. They don't have a purpose. When you find your purpose you never have to worry about being motivated again. You automatically know where you are going. Every morning your feet hit the deck and there is a clear mission of what your life is about.

The first step in finding your overall purpose is to discover what the Visionary Leader recognises as a higher level of motivation or purpose. This higher level is known as your Grand Purpose.

Everyone has the same Grand Purpose. It is this: the certain knowledge that *your primary mission is to grow and evolve.*

I have felt from an early age that my Grand Purpose is simply my personal evolution, that my task is to constantly grow. Any action that I take that leads me towards that Grand Purpose means that I am on track. Any action that leads me away from it means I am off track. It is that simple.

Let's say that you have reached a point in your journey where you absolutely know that the primary reason you are here on earth is to grow and evolve. You know that there is more to life than just existing. Congratulations, you have achieved step one of becoming more of a Visionary Leader.

Step 2: Recognising your unique direction

"While there is no vision, the people perish."

Proverbs 29. 18

Once you are clear about what your Grand Purpose is, you need to find your "vision", your unique way of living out your Grand Purpose in the world. Your vision is your gift to the world. It is something you were born to do. You will recognise it because it is your contribution to the world. It may be as a passionate artist who brings joy to people, or as a highly skilled waiter who makes diners feel comfortable and special. Each of us has a unique gift. This gift or purpose is inside each one of us waiting to be discovered. You don't have to invent it, because it is already there within you.

James Gleick in his book *Chaos* describes how scientists have demonstrated that when a fern leaf is curled up waiting to unfold, a template already exists for how that particular frond will look when it unravels. It is the same with each one of us. You hold within you a template, or a vision, of who you are and what you can become. Just as each fern is unique and an act of creation, so is your life. Your work lies in finding the courage to unfold into our potential.

Mahatma Ghandi dreamed of a liberated India that was free from British rule. That was his vision. Pursuing this vision shaped and forged Ghandi into one of the towering figures of the 20th century. His vision enabled him to grow and evolve, and move towards his Grand Purpose.

Your vision will usually present itself in one of two ways. It will most likely be something that you are extremely passionate about, or something that frightens you. Sometimes, both. *There are two kinds of fear.* The first is healthy fear, for example, being frightened of jumping out of a plane without a parachute. Healthy fear keeps us alive.

The second is obstructive fear, fear that you need to push through, fear that is merely an obstruction in your path.

Nelson Mandela felt a tremendous passion to help liberate his people. He also admits there were times when he felt afraid. However, he overcame his fear, which he recognised as an obstacle on his path, eventually becoming the leader of his country. By fulfiling his vision he took a giant step towards his own evolution. The experiences of his life, and his vision for a just society, transformed him from a shy student at school and university to a great leader honoured throughout the world.

When you choose a vision, it shapes you and allows you to grow, thus fulfiling your Grand Purpose of constant evolution.

If you feel that you have never found your "glove," your unique vision or career, don't despair. There was a period in my life when I thought I would never find mine. I would read articles about successful people who had found the work they were born to do. I thought they were extremely fortunate, and doubted I could be so lucky.

Having worked with thousands of people searching for their vision over the years, I believe there is only one way to find your vision: *you must be willing to commit yourself 100% to your vision before you know what it is.*

Yes, commit first. Why? Because you can set your own goals, but your vision is discovered. It is a gift from the Divine Force, that God energy that permeates us and the entire universe. You don't *choose* your Grand Purpose or vision, it is something you feel compelled to do. Perhaps your only choice is in actually doing it, for in reality, your vision chooses you.

Here is how it works. The Divine Force has a job that needs to be done, and needs someone to do it. If you aren't committed, why would it waste its energy on you when it could find somebody else for the job? Hey, after all, there are six billion people on the planet.

Let's say you are the head of a business and you interview twenty people for an important job. If someone comes into the office who isn't ready to commit to the work, would you give them the job?

Every day you are being interviewed by the Divine Force. That force knows your every whim and every intention. While you may temporarily fool yourself, the Divine Force is never fooled. It never judges you as right or wrong but perhaps at this moment in time, unready.

Commitment lies in the domain of the Achiever, which will be explored in the next chapter. You need this commitment to discover your vision and develop your Visionary Leader.

YOUR VISION EMPOWERS YOU

Visions do not have to be confined to career or a big vision out in the world. There are other visions that aid your evolution which work on a more emotional and personal level.

I remember Kimberley quite vividly. She was sitting up the front in a seminar, her quiet, intelligent face transfixed in concentration. We were talking about this very subject of finding a vision. Kimberley finally said, "I know that I am here to evolve, but I also know what holds me back from evolving."

Everyone could feel the tension in her voice as she continued. "I have been in a relationship now for several years. The person that I am with loves me very much. I know he is the right person for me but I have never committed to him or the relationship. In fact I have never really committed to anything in life and this is really holding me back. I feel as if life is passing me by and I am sitting on the sidelines, too frightened to really jump in."

Then Kimberley suddenly straightened, intently looking around the room, and said with total conviction, "Well I've had it, I have decided that I am really going to commit to this relationship. It scares the hell out of me and excites me all at the same time, but I know its what I have to do."

A few weeks later I received a wonderful letter from her saying how much her relationship had changed.

Making the decision to commit to her relationship was a specific vision that took Kimberley one step closer to her Grand Purpose. She knew it was the right decision because it was both scary and passionate.

Your Grand Purpose is a constant and continues, however your vision can change to fulfil your Grand Purpose.

A good way to think of how your Grand Purpose and your vision relate to each other is to imagine you are sitting in the pilot seat of a jet. The jet is currently parked on the runway in Paris. Deep down inside, you recognise that your Grand Purpose is to fly west. You decide to set a course to New York. Travelling westwards to New York is the vision that helps you move closer to your Grand Purpose. Once you arrive at New York, this vision is fulfiled. However, as your Grand Purpose is to fly west you need another vision, so you decide to go to San Francisco. Once you are there, your vision is complete but has your Grand Purpose been fulfiled? No, so you set out westwards for Tokyo.

Just as your destinations will change, your visions will change over time. Something that you were extremely passionate about ten years ago may no longer appeal to you today. In my case I realised that I had to leave a successful business. If I was to keep evolving, my vision had to change. As my passion for Real Estate diminished, my passion for "coming out" and speaking what I knew was growing. Fulfiling this vision helped me to keep pursuing my grand purpose.

When your Visionary Leader is well-developed, you become clear on what your vision is, and can recognise the difference between a true vision and a simple desire or wish for something. I wish I could sing as well as Andrea Bocelli, and I would love to play the guitar like Eric Clapton. The truth is, I'm not committed to these things because I don't have a strong enough motive. I don't have the motivation because I can't see how these talents would help me to evolve. They just don't fit into my Grand Purpose. However, when I look at Clapton playing that guitar it looks like an extension of himself. It's definitely his glove.

If you want to be wealthy and your only desire is to make a lot of money, this is unlikely to eventuate. Desiring money is not a strong vision. It has to dovetail with some other purpose, or the motivation will not be there. People who achieve great wealth are often asked whether their motivation is money. They usually reply by saying, "Yes, but more so I deeply wanted to make something of myself. To see if I could do it. It was a challenge."

Genuine passion is created by finding your Grand Purpose and discovering your unique vision.

Step 3: Finding your unique vehicle

"A musician must make music, an artist must paint, a poet must write if he is ultimately at peace with himself."

Abraham Maslow

THE VEHICLE

Once you are clear on your vision, you need to make it a reality by seeking out a vehicle. A Vehicle comprises the actions you undertake to fulfil your vision and, by extension, your Grand Purpose.

There are many different vehicles that will help you fulfil your Grand Purpose of constant evolution. You may, for example, have a vision to spiritually grow. Your vehicle to fulfil this may be to meditate or explore yourself more deeply.

In my own case, my vision is to empower myself and others. I do this by running seminars, writing books and producing audio tapes. My seminars, tapes and books are my vehicles.

If we return to the example of Ghandi, his vision was to liberate India from British rule. One of his vehicles was the great march he led across the country. At the time, the British had a monopoly on manufacturing salt in India and it was illegal for the citizens of India to make their own salt, a highly used commodity in the their lifestyle. Ghandi marched to the ocean, galvanising the Indian people against colonial rule, and in defiance of British law, made a small quantity of salt on the seashore. This march was just one of the vehicles that eventually led to the fulfilment of Ghandi's vision: an independent India.

Sometimes, driving your vehicle does not seem easy or straight forward. Let's say you have a vision to bring the story of an inspiring person you know to a wide audience. You choose as your vehicle to make a film about this person. The only problem is, you don't know the first thing about filmmaking. This doesn't mean that you have chosen the wrong vehicle, but it does mean that you have to set some goals. Goals are the tools that help you manifest your vehicle. For example, you might set a goal to learn about filmmaking by enrolling in a course. You might have a goal to meet other people in the business who can help you make your film by joining a filmmakers group. These goals help you to get your vehicle on the road to fulfiling your vision.

Once you know your Grand Purpose and have discovered your vision, you become clear about who you are and what you stand for. Standing firm in this knowledge, you become your own beacon and an inspiration for others to be who they really are.

This clarity of vision is important when it comes to choosing a vehicle. It can also save you a lot of time by preventing you from becoming confused or side-tracked from your unique path.

I was once approached to participate in a pyramid scheme money game. Like most of these games, eventually the people who are at the bottom lose out. I declined the invitation.

The game is illegal; however, that wasn't why I chose not to participate. The game was also, I believed, immoral, but again that was not the main reason why I didn't play–being righteous about other people's morals is boring and condescending. I didn't join in the game because I believed that it would diminish me as a person. It was that simple. I had a choice to grow and evolve or to be diminished. Playing this game was not a vehicle that would have fulfiled my Grand Purpose of evolving.

The key to finding your vision is to follow your heart. Go with your passion and acknowledge to yourself that you are here for a reason. The Divine Force has placed you here to fulfil a purpose. You are vital and important. When you realise this, more of your vision will reveal itself.

Grand Purpose, visions, and vehicles are central to the Visionary Leader. They are linked in the following way:

GRAND PURPOSE

|

VISION

|

VEHICLE

One way of illustrating these links, and the three steps involved in developing your Visionary Leader, is to imagine that you want to collect rainwater. Your Grand Purpose may be to quench your thirst, but your vision is to drink rainwater. Like your vision, rain descends from "on high". Now, if you want to collect the rain, you first have to go out and buy a bucket. The bucket is your vehicle. Buying the bucket is your goal. If you have committed yourself to your vision of drinking rainwater, whilst it is sunny, you will go out and buy the bucket and be ready for the next downpour. If you wait until it rains and then go to the store to buy a bucket, the rain storm may pass over before you get back.

AWAKENING YOUR INNER POWER

The second great quality of the Visionary Leader is Power

Very few words are as misunderstood as the word 'power'. Many people are frightened of power, often associating it with dictators or tyrants. We have all heard Lord Acton's saying "Power corrupts, absolute power corrupts absolutely," but is this really true? And what about the saying "Money is the root of all evil." There are many wealthy people accused of corruption and wrong doing. However, there are also many corrupt people who have neither money nor power. Power can make corruption more pervasive and visible, but corruption does not issue from power, it comes from a lack of integrity.

It is a curious thing with many of these pronouncements that if they are said often enough, they seem to be "facts". However, they are not facts, they are beliefs, and beliefs are not always true. Broad sweeping generalisations are dangerous. There are a lot of great people who are both wealthy and powerful. You need to be careful about which beliefs you take on board. Beliefs have an extreme influence on your behaviour and the way you operate in the world.

Let's look at the word "power." The Oxford Dictionary defines power as the "ability to do or act." Very simple. Nothing untoward about that. Let's break these words down. "To do or act" is the realm of the Achiever. It gets things done. That leaves the word "ability." What is it that gives you the ability to do something? For many people it is a sense of clarity of purpose, often coming from a clearly defined vision. Authentic power emanates from within. It doesn't seek to control others but allows you the freedom to be who you are. People who need to control others suffer from feelings of insecurity. That is not real power.

One common image of power is that of a stereotypical cigar smoking tycoon, but you don't have to be big and bombastic to emanate power. For example, Mother Teresa was humble, very quiet and only tiny in physical stature, but it was said that when she walked into a room she commanded attention just by her presence. She had power.

Nelson Mandela quoted Marianne Williamson when he spoke of this type of power during his inaugural speech as the new President of South Africa:

> *"Our deepest fear is not that we are inadequate, our deepest fear is that we are powerful beyond measure. It is our light, not our darkness, that frightens us. We ask ourselves: Who am I to be brilliant, gorgeous, talented and fabulous? Actually, who are you NOT to be. You are a child of God. Your playing small doesn't serve the world. There is nothing enlightened about shrinking so that other people won't feel insecure around you.*
>
> *We were born to make manifest the glory of God within us. It's not just in some of us, it is in everyone and as we let our own light shine we unconsciously give other people permission to do the same. As we are liberated from our own fear, our presence automatically liberates others."*

EMBRACING YOUR POTENTIAL

If you know someone who is lacking in power it is often because they don't have a clear vision of who they are or what they want to do. It can also be that they don't embrace their vision, but hide from their true potential. Often these people are falsely humble. They hold their energy in and appear invisible, like Sandra.

I remember the first time I met Sandra. She was sitting in the back row of a seminar. Sandra wore her dark hair tightly pulled across her head and fastened very sensibly in a hair clip. In fact, everything about Sandra was practical and sensible. It looked as though she hadn't let her hair down for years. Even though she was extremely intelligent, Sandra was very shy, quiet and withdrawn. She was in her twenties, but looked like she was going on forty.

What was Sandra doing? She was controlling herself. She was

violating her natural state of expanded power. How she appeared on the outside didn't match who she was on the inside.

The first thing I did with Sandra was ask her if she was happy being like that? She replied that she wasn't. She felt she would do anything to break out of her shell. So I put on some music and got Sandra to dance in front of the whole room. At first she was embarrassed but with the co-operation of the group, who were applauding and cheering her on, she gradually warmed to the task and ended up leading everyone in a dance.

What Sandra did was take a risk. Visionary Leaders who utilise their inner power do not base their lives on feeling safe. They take risks.

Our lives are full of risks. Even falling in love is a risk. After all, there are no guarantees your heart won't be broken. There will always be a point where you will have to choose to play it safe, or take the risk.

I remember playing "peekaboo" with my baby daughter. As I came out from a hiding place to say "boo," she broke into fits of uninhibited giggling. Her whole face lit up and her body shook with laughter. There was such an innocence and natural joy. In that moment, I felt so much love for her that I could barely contain it. And then I felt vulnerable. This little person held my life in the palm of her hand. I realised that if anything happened to her I would feel devastated. I had a choice: I could protect myself by not allowing myself to love so completely, or I could take a risk. I opened myself even more to be completely in the moment, even though I could feel the fear.

If you close down and put up protection barriers, you diminish yourself. If you want to follow your own unique purpose there will always be some risk. Rather than shrinking from risk, you need to embrace it. I'm not talking about being foolhardy, I'm talking about going for what you want.

Anita Roddick, founder of The Body Shop, was, by her own admission, a bit of a hippie. She took a risk in setting up her first store by taking out a large bank loan. Her risk paid off and The Body Shop is now a flourishing business empire.

Amelia Earhart became a household name when she flew over 2000 miles from Newfoundland to Ireland in the 1930s and became the first woman to fly solo across the Atlantic. Millions of people were inspired by the risk she took.

The Indian saint Mira Bai was a royal princess who took a tremendous risk. She defied the ironclad caste system by choosing Ravidas, a low caste cobbler, as her spiritual teacher. Despite enduring constant criticism and invoking the ire of the palace, she went on to write some of India's most beautiful, devotional prose.

To take risks and utilise your inner power is to inspire yourself and others.

INSPIRING YOURSELF AND OTHERS

The ability to inspire is derived from combining the two great qualities of the Visionary Leader, purpose and power. When you have a vision and combine that with your inner power you become an inspiration to yourself and others. People who base their entire lives on safety cannot lead others because they cannot inspire them.

Aung San Suu Kyi, who was imprisoned by the Burmese military after her party won 82 percent of the vote in the national elections, reminds us of our own Visionary Leader. In awarding her the Nobel Peace Prize, Professor Sejersted said:

> *"We ordinary people, I believe, feel that with her courage and her high ideals Aung San Suu Kyi brings out something of the best in us. We feel we need precisely her sort of person in order to retain our faith in the future. That is what gives her such power as a symbol, and that is why any ill-treatment of her feels like a violation of what we have most at heart... Knowing she is there gives us confidence and faith in the power of good."*

Martin Luther King and Mahatma Ghandi were also risk takers. This is why they were able to inspire millions of people.

It is not just great leaders who fulfil the role of a Visionary Leader by being inspirational risk takers. I am inspired by anyone who stands up for what they believe in, taking a risk in the face of popular opinion, such as the normally reserved person at work who takes a stand against something they perceive to be unjust.

THE VISIONARY LEADER'S TOOLKIT

CREATING NEW POSSIBILITIES

A study was once carried out in which teachers were given the IQ of each student in their class. As you would expect, the more "gifted" students who had higher IQs performed better than the other, less "gifted" students. However, the teachers were deliberately given the wrong information. The students who had supposedly high IQs actually had normal IQs. Because the teachers had an expectation that certain students would perform very well, the students responded. The teachers believed these students to be gifted and the children expanded into this potentiality.

True Visionary Leaders takes this quality to another level. They will "hold the possibility" of someone becoming who they are, well before that person has arrived at that state. They have the ability to see their own and others' maximum potential, to recognise the template that they and others will grow into.

In reality, we are all gifted. "Holding the possibility" is about looking at yourself and others and seeing them at their highest potential or expanded state. Most of us are trained to see people as they are, rather than what they could become, but we are all constantly changing, learning and evolving. Holding someone in past pictures does not help them. Imagine saying to a new-born baby that all they will ever be is a baby. No sane adult would ever do that because they know the baby will grow. A parent sees the baby as it is, but also knows the baby will become a child, who will become a teenager, and so on.

To be a great leader to yourself and others you need to know the difference between the present and the possibility. Seeing others in the present is about recognising who they are right now. Seeing the possibility is recognising their potential. For example, letting someone who is illiterate prepare your tax return is not recognising their current skill. However, believing that they could never be in a position to prepare a tax return only serves to hold that person in a box of narrow possibilities.

It is exactly the same with yourself. You need to be able to see yourself in the *present* and also hold the *possibility* of who you could become. Who is the person that determines the difference between where you are now and where you want to go? It is you.

When I first saw Sandra "in the present," I saw a painfully shy person who was frightened of speaking up. However, I instantly recognised the real Sandra underneath the "act"–a vibrant human being who desperately wanted to break out of her shell. Instead of seeing Sandra only in the present, I saw the possibility. So did Sandra, and that is what enabled her transformation. She saw the possibility and recognised her true nature.

MASTERING SELF COMMAND

Why do people such as Sandra avoid embracing their power? Why do millions of people live lives of limitation? I have met countless people who seem to unconsciously spend a great part of their life drawing in all their energy as close to their skin as possible, controlling themselves. It seems they are almost on a quest to shrink. Then there are many others who pretend to be outgoing but inside feel very contracted. I searched for a long time to understand why this phenomenon occurs. I believe it is due to the misunderstanding of two concepts: "command" and "control."

Truly great leaders have command. Command is a form of inner mastery, a combination of being centred and powerful. When you are in command of your inner resources, you feel expanded and poised. Someone who is in control however, makes choices based on fear. The classic "control freak" fears that their whole world will collapse if they don't control themselves and the everything around them.

Think of a conductor leading an orchestra. When they are in command, they are poised and centred, confident in their abilities and those around them. They *direct* each member of the orchestra rather than *control* them. The musicians know that the conductor believes in them and so they give everything to the music.

Imagine there are two parts of you. One is an inner part which has the ability to express whatever you are feeling and thinking in the moment. The other is an outer part which has the ability to control what you are feeling and thinking. When someone is in control, they deliberately stop the internal process of expression. In fact, a lot of people are so used to controlling their inner world that when you ask them what they are feeling, they can only answer, "I don't know." They are most likely telling the truth. Control may have become such an ingrained habit that they may not have any idea what is happening on the inside.

Other people control themselves out of fear. Sandra was so frightened of what people thought of her that she kept everything in, including her energy.

Having command is a totally different, expanded state. It is essential to master the state of "command" in order to embrace more of who you are and become a Visionary Leader.

EXERCISE: PERSONAL EXPANSION

Let us look at the ability to command your own sense of personal expansion. Have you ever met anyone who seems to have a large presence? They walk into a room and command attention merely by being there. They seem to be in command of themselves and comfortable with who they are.

It is easy to develop this ability. Let's try an exercise. Sit in a comfortable chair. Begin by relaxing yourself. Take some deep breaths into your lower diaphragm. Now, just by using the power of your own will, imagine that your personal energy is expanding out into the room, that you are getting bigger and bigger. See if you can stretch your energy, your sense of presence way out.

Now try the opposite. Imagine you are hiding from someone and you are pulling your energy closer and closer to yourself, making yourself smaller and smaller. Think shrink. Now try expanding again, then shrinking and then expanding.

If you practice this exercise every day you will begin to notice something very interesting. The more relaxed you are, and the less fear you have, the easier it is to do. In fact if you are very relaxed and in a state of no fear you will naturally expand out and out, without using any willpower. It will just naturally happen. This is authenticity. Being who you are without using force. It is the most wonderful feeling.

AUTHENTICITY

Let's look at the word authentic. It comes from the Greek "authentikos", meaning "genuine". If you don't completely know who you are and what you stand for, how can you ever hope to be you own author and write your own, unique life script? As Shakespeare said, "This above all, to thine own self be true".

Until you become yourself, you will be the wrong person looking for the right thing. Imagine if I asked a stranger to design a life for you. This stranger was going to design your spiritual, mental and emotional makeup. They would have complete autonomy over what you want in life, your career and your unique direction. How confident would you be that this stranger could come up with the right design? Not confident at all, right? Unfortunately, this is the condition of a vast number of people. They are a stranger to themselves and so can never discover their unique destiny.

When you allow yourself to be who you really are inside, to truly know yourself, there is a tremendous sense of freedom. You feel liberated and alive. Now, think of what liberation and freedom feel like. Do these states feel contracted or expanded? Expanded, of course. That is the nature of expansion: freedom to be who you are, in every given moment; to be in command of your life, living life truly on your own terms; going your own way, living your own path, setting your own rules. You are not contracted and "in control", living a life based on what you *think* you should be doing.

Being "in command," as opposed to being "in control," is completely different to being "out of control". If you want to get a good idea of what being "out of control" is about, just watch a group of young people who are celebrating and have had too much alcohol. They may be expressing everything they are thinking and feeling, but they have no command over that expression. It is all coming out without any filters.

Compare this with truly great actors or singers who are in command. When Anthony Hopkins acts, for example, he is completely in command. He goes to the depth of his core, his inner feeling, and channels that expression in line with the character he is portraying. His inner world is uncontrolled which allows him to tap the wellspring of his creativity. However, he leaves out what is unnecessary.

CREATING TRUE FREEDOM FOR YOURSELF AND OTHERS

A wise Visionary Leader will lead people by utilising command rather than control. Leading by controlling others produces two effects: people rebel or they become compliant. Essentially they act against you or they suppress themselves unwillingly to go along with your choices. By leading others utilising command, you sidestep both these reactions. Raising children provides good examples of these two types of responses.

Many years ago I went out to dinner with my wife Annie and my two teenage children. As the dinner progressed, the children started acting in what I believed was an inappropriate fashion, speaking loudly and generally misbehaving. At first I was puzzled because usually they had a good sense of what was appropriate. Pretty soon though, I started to feel embarrassed. People at other tables began to cast disapproving *"Hmmm"* glances our way. I quickly tried to clamp down on their behaviour, trying to control them. I was operating from a fear of what people thought of me. In response, my children rebelled. Their behaviour worsened.

At this point my wife turned to me. "Brendan, you seem very tense. Do you think you are in control here?"

It was a good question. Was I in control? I realised that she was right. Internally I felt uptight and contracted and was operating from fear. I decided to join my children and start acting up myself, not in an outrageous way, but enough to get their attention. The result was that in less then two minutes they completely settled down. In fact, my son said, "Hey Dad, chill out will you, you're embarrassing me."

The responses of rebellion or compliance can be illustrated by what I call "the scales of control". On one side is the force of Rebellion, and on the other side is the force of Compliance.

Let's look at a mythical family: The Harrisons. John and Marjory Harrison are regarded as pillars of society. They are the well-meaning parents of Julian and Sarah. John and Marjory love their children very much.

Being well aware of the drug problem, they are very frightened of what could become of their children. They adopt an extremely strict regime with Julian and Sarah, and carefully screen all their friends. Although they may be pursuing the right actions and choices for their children, they are operating from a place of fear rather than concern.

If they were in command, they would be concerned for their children and steer them in the right direction. I believe it is the responsibility of every parent to give direction. This is the function of The Visionary Leader: to give direction, to be in command. However, Mr and Mrs Harrison are not only motivated by the fear of the drug culture. They are essentially frightened that their children may not be successful, that Julian and Sarah may not live up to their expectations.

As Julian and Sarah grow up, a distinct pattern emerges. Julian turns into a rebel and Sarah turns into a very conservative young woman. Julian starts taking drugs and joins a heavy metal band. Sarah joins the bank. They both think they are acting out of choice, but in reality, Julian is acting out of rebellion and Sarah is acting out of compliance.

Real freedom is something else. It is the midpoint between Rebellion and Compliance. It isn't about "not doing" or "should be" doing. It is about doing something because you genuinely love to do it, because you recognise it as your unique direction.

The states of rebellion and compliance are completely different from the state of being in command. When you are in command you experience true freedom, the incredible feeling of knowing who you really are. You are then free to express what you want in the world. Freedom is the ability to be in command and express yourself in accordance with your unique individual makeup.

Much of the leadership that I see in families and the business world is control leadership. Control leadership allows a person, family or company to survive, and in many cases to do quite well. However, command leadership allows organisations and their individuals to flourish.

In the last few years of my Real Estate career, I defied popular convention by adopting a command leadership style. I hired people who were all close friends and made the primary intention of the business to be an arena where people could become empowered. I took the emphasis away from making money and created an atmosphere where people could expand into their maximum potential. This was virtually unheard of, but validated my belief that a command style of leadership is not only more fulfiling, it is more effective.

I have explained this concept to other leaders. Some of them understand it and some of them don't. Those that don't fully comprehend the concept think they can adopt a command style of leadership as a strategy. However, command style has to come from the heart. It has to be a genuine desire to see people fulfil their potential.

Whether you have played golf, surfed a big wave or walked a tightrope, you will know how essential it is to be in command rather than control. With all these activities, and many more, it is essential you stay relaxed and fluid. If you are locked up and controlled, then you are destined to hit a wayward shot, wipe out on a wave or lose your balance on the high wire.

TRAITS THAT SELF-SABOTAGE

AVOIDING THE "SMALL REASONS" TRAP

What stops you from pursuing your unique vision or dream? The answer is what I call "Small Reasons".

Just as the urge to eat and drink is an instinct, your Grand Purpose for living is also an instinct. You have certain impulses so that you survive **and** thrive. Notice I said survive and thrive. You are not meant to just exist but also to bloom.

If you want to satisfy your hunger and thirst instincts, all you need to do is eat bread and water. However this is not a diet that will allow you to thrive. Similarly, there are millions of people working in jobs that satisfy their instinct to survive by providing income, but the instinct to thrive remains unsatisfied. They don't really like what they are doing. They are on the equivalent of bread and water rations and are not being spiritually or emotionally nourished. They are not thriving.

You may think that slavery in the western world is dead, but this is not the case. Slavery is alive and well. In fact, the slavery that exists today in our culture, is even more insidious than it was in the 1800s because most people do not even see they are in slavery. There are no external slave masters, but a huge number of people are self-imprisoned. Many are in life situations, relationships or careers that do not bring them happiness or satisfaction. They are their own slave master, controlling themselves, holding themselves in. They suppress their Grand Purpose and unique vision out of insecurity and a fear of not being safe and accepted. They are being driven by "Small Reasons", such as "I have to pay the bills," "What will my friends and colleagues think?", "Will I jeopardise my chances of promotion?"

Now, Small Reasons are important in life. You need to pay the bills and handle the details but Small Reasons do not make up a vision. Small Reasons relate to management, and this shouldn't be confused with Visionary Leadership. Management refers to handling the day to day running of your life. Visionary Leadership is the dream that inspires you. A manager of a family or a business looks after all the very important details, the Small Reasons. A leader creates the vision. Many politicians are uninspiring because they are managers rather than leaders.

> *"Nothing has a stronger influence psychologically on their environment, and especially on their children, than the unlived life of the parents."*
>
> CARL JUNG

The impact of Small Reasons can be seen in the following story. There are countless people who secretly struggle to find fulfilment, and I have met many like Mary and Jonathan.

Mary and Jonathan had been in a relationship for seven years. Mary worked as a retail manager with a large supermarket chain. Jonathan was climbing the career ladder in a firm of architects. When they first got together the relationship was full of passion and they both felt alive. Jonathan had always nursed a dream that after finishing his degree he would take two years off and sail around the world. Mary was attracted to his heroic sense of adventure for she had dreams and a vision of her own. She loved interior design and wanted to start her own company. They decided, however, to put their dreams on hold for just a little while and do the sensible thing. They would save up and buy a house.

Seven years had gone by. Mary often felt that she had missed her opportunity. Working in a supermarket was not quite her. It didn't really feel like it was what she was meant to be doing with her life.

In his quieter moments, Jonathan wondered what the hell he was doing in the architectural firm. He had very little in common with his colleagues and he felt like an outsider. It was as if he was scrambling to get to the top of a hill. The only problem was, it was the wrong hill.

When Mary and Jonathan talked about how they both felt stuck, there seemed too much pressure to change. Jonathan believed that if he left the firm their income would stop. He reasoned that their lifestyle would suffer and their friends would look down on them. He didn't like the thought of not being able to keep up. Mary wasn't willing to take the risk of giving up her job. They could lose the house, which would make her feel extremely insecure. He worried about what people would think of him, and she was willing to give up her dreams for the sake of security.

Both Mary and Jonathan were dominated by Small Reasons. They were not living with a Grand Purpose, but rather, with a whole host of Small Reasons. While they were both outgoing and well liked by all their friends, deep down they both felt something was missing in their lives. They didn't feel as alive as they used to. They did not feel inspired nor did their partner inspire them.

Their relationship was suffering too. Their friends thought they had it all together but they both knew that they were becoming more distant and unfulfilled. They often felt as though they were just existing rather than thriving. Did this mean they should split up? Not at all. They simply needed to find their individual visions and thus become more personally fulfiled. When they are personally fulfiled they feel happier and thus are able to more fully love and support their partner and themselves.

A DREAM DENIED AND REKINDLED

It is a tragedy when I see people deliberately slow, alter or stop their unfolding, their journey to follow their vision. It was particularly difficult to watch my daughter fall prey to Small Reasons.

Ever since my daughter was at high school, she had nursed a dream of being involved in the performing arts. One night she came home from school, walked into the lounge room, and stood in front of the big open window that looked out onto the tropical garden. I was reading on the lounge, and she waited until she had my full attention before making an announcement.

"Dad, I've decided that I am going to forget acting. When I go to university next year I will study to become a school teacher."

Now, if that was what she really wanted to do from her heart it would have been no problem. As I listened to her though, it sounded like she had as much passion to be a teacher as someone volunteering to stand in front of a firing squad.

She went on to say, "Everybody at school tells me there is no secure future in film or theatre. I just think that if I can get a secure job first, then later on I can try out for something in the acting world."

We talked about it for a while, but her mind was made up. "Chalk one up for the dream killers," I thought to myself, as I pondered the fate of the millions of people who have given up their dream to do the "sensible, practical thing".

Experience has taught me that sometimes you just have to let people follow their own course, so I sat by as my daughter entered university. As the months wore on in that first year she grew more and more unhappy, struggling to find some meaning in her choice of subjects. One day, about six months into the year, she clambered into my car with her own portable rain cloud sitting above her head, looking sad and bewildered.

I turned to her and asked, "So how long do you plan on enduring this?" She burst into tears and slumped into my arms. The next couple of days we talked a lot.

I said to her, "I understand that you feel confused, but the most important thing is for you to be happy. You are the only person who can steer your boat. Make a choice to please yourself, not me or anyone else."

A few days later she switched courses to the performing arts, and the smiles and passion returned. Right now she is in the middle of producing her first film. She is working extraordinarily long hours for little financial reward, but she loves every minute of it.

Small Reasons may seem sensible and practical from one point of view, but in reality they are impediments to fulfiling your Visionary Leader. Let me return to the analogy I used earlier of collecting water. It went like this: your Grand Purpose is to quench your thirst; your vision is to drink rainwater; your bucket is your vehicle, the means of making your vision a reality. Some people have big strong buckets, others have leaky ones. When you've got holes in your bucket, it's hard to collect anything. Small Reasons create holes in your bucket and allow your vision to drain away.

THE ONE-DIMENSIONAL VISIONARY LEADER

"Regret for the things we did can be tempered by time; it is regret for the things that we did not do that is inconsolable."

SYDNEY J. HARRIS

I was in a cab heading to the airport not long ago. The driver was a man in his mid fifties who had an aura of frustration and despair about him. He looked like a person who was nearing the end of a train ride and approaching the final station called regret.

We started chatting and I asked him about his day. As the conversation began to get a little deeper, he told me of a vision he had nursed for many years. It was the one thing that would finally get him out from behind the steering wheel of a cab and into something fulfiling. I listened as he talked about what seemed to be the last thread of hope in his life.

Finally I asked, "What do you need to make it happen?"

He replied, "I'm just waiting for my lucky break and someone to come along who can fund it".

I got the feeling that he was hoping that one day Bill Gates or Rupert Murdoch would climb in the back of his cab and just pull out a cheque book.

This taxi driver may have had a vision, but without having some of the other quintessential elements in balance, his dream remained dormant.

The person whose only developed element is the Visionary Leader, needs the Achiever to make that vision happen. Otherwise it will probably remain just that – a vision. Another word for a vision is an apparition, something that isn't real. To turn a vision into reality, rather than an apparition, you need the Achiever.

Without the Poet, the Visionary Leader runs the risk of jeopardising their relationships with family and friends by stumbling over their own arrogance. History is littered with the corpses of Visionary Leaders who, puffed up by their own importance, made decisions that spelled their doom.

The Visionary Leader also needs the wisdom of the Sage to warn them of pitfalls on the way to fulfiling their vision. Many a fortune has been lost because someone denied their intuition in favour of an "I can do anything" attitude.

THE EXTRAORDINARY VISIONARY LEADER

What is the maximum potential of the Visionary Leader? What is the ideal state they aspire to, and what feelings does this state give them?

If the Visionary Leader was a peak that you could climb, then the summit of that mountain would have a sign on it that reads, "Congratulations, you have reached the stage where you no longer care what people think of you."

At this level, you are so grounded in who you are, what you stand for and what your vision is, that eliciting popular opinion is no longer relevant. There is a tremendous freedom in this state. When someone arrives at this place, they emanate a powerful presence.

One of the biggest fears that people have is the fear of ostracism, the fear of being excluded from their particular community. Some people would twist themselves in knots rather than be ridiculed. Visionary Leaders, however, are willing to operate in "non-agreement". This is a state where they are willing to live their unique way of life and genuinely not care what people think.

When you can operate in non-agreement you harness a huge amount of energy. This energy is often channelled into self censorship. Wearing the right thing, saying the right thing, doing the right thing. Absolutely exhausting. When you can just be yourself, you free yourself.

The Visionary Leader sits comfortably in their own skin.

Harriet Tubman was a great example of a Visionary Leader who operated in non-agreement. She was someone who was in command of her own life and her own direction. Born into slavery in 1820 in Bucktown, Maryland, she made a daring dash to freedom at the age of twenty-nine. Her mission in life (her vision) became helping other slaves to freedom through what was known as "The Underground Railway", and hence she was known to slaves as "Moses".

The Underground Railway wasn't a real railway, but rather a network of people and routes that led the oppressed into the free states such as Philadelphia and Ohio. In an ingenious system, a code was developed where railroad terms were used. Places to hide were called stations. People like Harriet who led these slaves were known as conductors.

Of course all of this was considered a crime, and the risks Harriet and the people who worked with her took were considerable. Despite the dangers, Harriet made over nineteen trips ferrying people to freedom, all of which were successful.

Tubman was not only a leader of others, but crucially, she was a visionary leader to herself first, by escaping into freedom in 1849. It is essential that you know who you are, so that you can lead yourself. Lead yourself first, then others can, and will, follow.

THE ACHIEVER

"I believe in challenges so great you know they are going to stretch you."

SIR EDMUND HILLARY, 47 YEARS AFTER FIRST ASCENDING EVEREST

ACHIEVING THE IMPOSSIBLE

It was just before midnight on July 30, 1997. Most of the village of Thredbo, a quiet ski resort in Australia, was asleep. Being the middle of winter, it was literally freezing. No one had any idea that in minutes one of Australia's most tragic disasters was about to occur.

High above the village, a water pipe had slowly been leaking, and over a period of months had saturated the earth beneath it. Without any warning a huge landslide started, destroying a ski lodge. The combined debris of the earth and that first lodge were to hit a second building, Bimbadeen Lodge, with a staggering ferocity. In less than one minute the entire area was reduced to rubble, earth and jagged concrete blocks. Nineteen people, mostly local staff, were buried under the wreckage.

The next day a media armada descended on the shocked village. Hardened media veterans were visibly moved by the tragedy. It was believed there were survivors under the tons of rubble, but it was a race against time. Not only was the site unstable, but the temperatures were dipping down to below zero. Most of those buried were, at best, dressed in pyjamas.

Stuart Diver, a ski instructor, was one of those trapped under the wreckage. At the moment of impact he had grabbed his wife, Sally's, hand. Moments later he realised she was dead. He was trapped in a tiny air pocket surrounded by rubble and concrete, dressed only in a pair of shorts and a soaking wet, thin cotton sheet to cover his legs.

As he lay there amidst the rubble a quiet, fierce anger slowly built up inside him as he realised his wife had died. He said later that it was partly this anger and the intention to live that enabled him to endure.

Stuart hung on for over thirty five hours in freezing conditions before he was discovered. Then came the arduous task of bringing him to the surface without collapsing his fragile tomb. The whole nation watched breathlessly, praying that at least this one courageous human being would be spared a tragic end.

Rescue workers moved at an agonisingly slow pace, constantly in fear of collapsing the rubble, knowing that no one could survive these conditions for much longer. More than sixty hours after he was first buried, a huge cheer rippled around the mountain as Stuart was finally brought to safety.

Stuart Diver is the lone survivor of the Thredbo disaster. A genuine hero. Although unassuming, he is an extraordinary human being and an incredible Achiever.

THE ACHIEVER'S BLUEPRINT

"A mighty flame followeth a tiny spark"

DANTE

The element associated with the Achiever is fire. It is the purifying fire that burns straight towards the goal. We often use the metaphor of fire when referring to the intention of the Achiever. Someone may be impassioned by a "fire in the belly", or a "burning desire". When they are really committed to a mission, they might say, "I'm on fire!", or "I feel fired up about this!"

Whether you are Karrie Webb or Tiger Woods on the golf course, working on a big business project or burning the midnight oil to get in a term paper, it is the fire of the Achiever that makes it happen. Achievers are tenacious, steadfast, determined and persistent. Like the element of fire, the Achiever burns its way to victory.

Achievers see the world as a place of challenge and an arena in which to test themselves. Enter the gladiators of the sports track and the business world. Anything that takes drive to be successful will see our Achievers crowding around trying to out compete each other, whether it be at chess or ice hockey, or setting up an orphanage. There is nothing they like more than a challenge, except when they win. They *love* that.

Achievers use the internal mechanism of competition to measure any action they are engaged in. If they are on a mission, they will evaluate how they are doing by comparing themselves to others or asking themselves if they are living up to their own standards. This evaluation spurs them on to their goal. It is their greatest blessing and their greatest curse. It is a blessing because this evaluation can lift them to higher and higher goals. But it can be a curse because sometimes it gives them no peace. As soon as they have arrived at their destination, they move on to the next goal.

The Achiever lives by a certain set of internal standards, and if they are not living up to these standards they will never be satisfied. Notice the word is *satisfied* rather than *happy*. Their happiness may be short-lived because their focus shifts to the next goal. Essentially they are *outcome driven.* They only see the achievement of the mission, (which is why they need the balance of the Poet, as will be discussed later in this chapter). However, this drive and commitment to outcomes is essential in the pursuit of their ambitions.

Achievers are often one-directional in their approach to life: "get out of my way I'm coming through". There are a few people out there who wear the tyre marks of an Achiever on a mission. Achievers believe in getting the job done above all else. Diplomacy comes later on their priority list. They want people around them who are doers.

As a result, those who work or live with Achievers can find it difficult to live up to their high expectations.

INTENTION

The Achiever is the key to unlocking all of the other elements and achieving the Quintessence. Whether you want a better relationship, financial success or spiritual attainment, it is the Achiever that creates the momentum.

Mother Teresa was a great example of the Quintessence, combining all the five elements. She had the determined will of the Achiever, the realistic dream of the Visionary Leader, the love and compassion of the Poet, and the wisdom and perception of the Sage, combined with a powerful spiritual presence. She said of her own spiritual journey, "It depends on God and myself – on God's grace and my will. The first step to becoming is to will it."

The first step in everything is to will it. If you want to pick up a plate from a shelf, you first have to will or intend it happening. If you decide to travel to Hawaii on vacation, you first have to intend it. *Intention means applying the force of the mind to a decision.* Intention is not just an idle curiosity, it is a committed desire. Intention is the mother of action and plays a large part in awakening all the elements. Intention is also the watchword of the Achiever.

RESPECT

Achievers have a unique value system. They primarily seek respect – from others and from themselves. The only way they can respect themselves is if they are living up to their own high standards. Many Achievers rank respect even more important than love. The reason for this is that Achievers are driven by the desire to constantly be at their edge. Their closest friends will be people they respect. In fact, the only way to ever become close to an Achiever is to first of all win their respect.

A die-hard Achiever will evaluate people by what they have done or achieved. They may even overlook some serious character flaw in an individual if that person has achieved something momentous. Achievers abhor weakness and seek to live life on the edge.

AWAKENING YOUR INNER FIRE

THE FIRST GREAT QUALITY OF THE ACHIEVER IS *COMMITMENT*

Mastering commitment is the first step in maximising your Achiever. Commitment is that powerful state when all your energies are focused on a single issue. You are clear, on target and alive. Commitment is the arrow-like force that emanates from deep within and drives your outcome to victory.

Commitment is the force that prevents you from becoming sidetracked. The Achiever, like the arrow, only knows one direction – straight towards the target. However, if that arrow comes from an archer who is distracted, it could land anywhere.

The joys of material success, a great relationship or strong spiritual union only come through commitment. I have met people who never commit to anyone or anything because they feel that person or situation will constrain them in some way. Others don't commit because they are waiting for something better to come along. What about deciding to commit yourself anyway?

Let's say your current job is washing dishes, but you know deep down that you want to be a great singer. While you're dish washing why not commit to it fully? Hey, you're there anyway, you might as well go for it. There's something about commitment that creates opportunities.

Commitment heralds magic.

If you meet a stranger in the street and are committed to being there fully in the moment with that person, you never know what could arise. It could lead you in a whole new direction. From one conversation, you might start a new career, relationship or business venture. When you commit yourself, even in ordinary moments, it is equivalent to wearing a neon sign that says "I can do the extraordinary".

Unwavering commitment is the rarefied domain of the Achiever. It creates focus, drive and a fierce determined will. It is the Achiever's highest form of charisma.

FINDING COMMITMENT

Three hundred years after the death of Gailileo, one of the most brilliant minds of our era was born. Stephen Hawking is famous for his scientific achievements, however his extraordinary career only eventuated after a strange twist of events.

At the age of twenty he was extremely bored with life. Although in good health and showing great intellectual promise, he felt that there really wasn't anything worth doing in life. There was nothing that inspired him to excel.

Not long after this, Hawking's father noticed that Stephen seemed to be getting uncharacteristically clumsy and insisted that he seek medical attention. After two weeks of testing, the doctors became evasive and the first waves of real apprehension began. Eventually Stephen's worst fears were confirmed when it was revealed that he had an incurable motor neurone disease that would probably kill him within a few years.

Hawking was shocked and stunned. At first all that went through his mind was, "How could something like this happen to me? Why should I be cut off in the prime of my life?" He felt depressed, with nothing to look forward to except a very uncertain future.

After a period of hospitalisation, he had a very powerful dream that he was going to be executed. The dream made him realise that if he were reprieved, there were a lot of worthwhile things he could do. Later he experienced another powerful dream that recurred several times, in which he sacrificed his life to save others. He began to feel that if he was going to die, why not do some good? While Hawking outlived the doctor's early predictions of a short life expectancy, what did die was his former lethargy to life. Even with the cloud of death hanging over his head, he found to his great surprise that he was enjoying life more than ever before. A new commitment for his work emerged within him.

Professor Hawking overcame tremendous odds through a quiet smouldering commitment. With a mountain of obstacles in his path, his inner conviction led him to scale the heights of scientific achievement, and become the recipient of twelve honorary degrees.

FROM PROCRASTINATION TO SUCCESS

THE FOUR RUNGS ON THE LADDER OF COMMITMENT

1: TAKING AN INTEREST

"He that lives upon hope will die fasting"

BENJAMIN FRANKLIN

The first and lowest level of commitment is interest, a desire to have something. Let's take the analogy of a journey to illustrate this. You are interested in going away somewhere for a weekend vacation, and so you climb into your parked car in the garage. As you sit in the car, you dream of that beautiful place up the road, just by the lake. It's an exclusive little hideaway, owned by people who are devoted to looking after your every need. You know about the hideaway because your neighbours told you what a great time they had there last weekend. Unfortunately, all you do is sit in the car dreaming about going away.

This first level of commitment is important, but problems arise when you get stuck in Level 1, when you can't seem to get out of the garage. Similarly, if you are on a personal and spiritual journey and get stuck at Level 1, you may believe that personal and spiritual change is a good idea and fantasise about one day becoming the person of your dreams, but that's all it remains – a fantasy.

The pitfall with Level 1 is that taking an interest in something can render it optional, you don't *need* it to happen. Being stuck in the car in the garage is a lot like being stuck in your head, *thinking* about what you would like to have happen in your life. Still, this is a better position to be in than those who have given up all hope of ever having anything good happen in their lives, like some of the street dwellers we see in our cities.

Some people have so lost hope that they can't even manage to make the journey to the garage. However, hope in itself can be a trap. There is an old Chinese saying, "Abandon all hope," warning that if you rely on hope, you may never actually do anything. There are plenty of people out there who believe that "one day" their ship will come in. I have met quite a few who firmly believe that "one day" they will win the lottery and all their dreams will come true. Hey, anything is possible, but I wouldn't want to count on it.

I had an opportunity to witness first hand how people operate at Level 1. Many years ago I was asked to be a guest speaker at a wealth creation program. What happened that night became a revelation in how I perceived people's abilities to determine their destiny. It was a lesson in how people stay stuck in Level 1, hoping that one day things will change.

When I entered the room the participants of the program were in an extremely motivated state. Everybody was either on their chairs, dancing or giving each other high fives. They were all moving to the beat of the song "I want to be rich". I love a good party and joined in, however, even though the atmosphere was electric, it felt to me that something was not quite right.

As everybody sat down, the presenters asked me to come to the front of the room. I could feel the expectation as I walked down the aisle. I turned to face a host of eager faces. Everyone was waiting for the pearls of wisdom to roll off my tongue.

"Let me ask you," I began. "What is this program about?"

The participants, who were more than half way through the event, were very clear on the subject.

"To create wealth and have financial independence," several voices chorused.

"Can't argue with that," I replied. "How many of you are committed to being wealthy and financially independent?" Every hand in the room shot up.

Many presenters would have moved on from there, but I asked the same question again.

"How many of you are committed to being wealthy and financially independent?"

Once more all the hands went up, this time even more vigorously than before.

After that I kept on repeating the same question over and over. At first people were puzzled. Had I lost the plot or was I auditioning for a role as Long John Silver's parrot? Finally, a big Polynesian who was sitting at the back of the room rose to speak. He was literally a mountain of a man and commanded an incredible presence. The room hushed as he stood there.

He looked directly at me and said, "Brendan, I thought I was extremely committed but you've got me thinking. The truth is, what means more to me than anything is family. I've always wanted more money but I've never really committed to it."

I looked at him and said, "That's okay. At least now you know what you are committed to."

Every person in the room got a chance to speak. At the end of the night there were two people in that group who, beyond a shadow of a doubt were committed to financial independence. Guess what? Those two already *were* financially independent.

That night I learned the difference between casually wanting something and *having* to have something.

2: PLEASING OTHERS – EXTERNAL COMMITMENT

The second level of commitment is external commitment. This refers to making commitments based on what people think of you. It is commitment derived from external sources. This is an important and sometimes necessary level, but as with Level 1, problems arise when you get stuck in it. Let's say that you have promised to deliver a report by a certain time. Your motivation for completing the report is based on the fact that if you don't get it in on time the report will be rejected and you will lose favour with your boss. This motivation is not a bad thing, in fact it is a good initial step. However, you need to recognise that it is coming from fear – fear of what your boss will think, fear of getting fired or fear of not getting that promotion. Level 2 will lead you to make commitments based on how you want people to perceive you.

Let's return to the analogy of our journey to a luxurious destination. Being at Level 2 is like getting in the car in your garage and driving somewhere that you really didn't want to go to in the first place. You had your heart set on going to that cute hideaway by the lake, but now you are driving to the cinema to see *Attack of the Space Gorillas* because your friend wants you to meet her there.

Some people make commitments because they just don't know how to say no. For example, going to a party when you're over tired because you don't want to offend anyone, or joining a charity organisation because it is perceived by others as a noble endeavour. Operating from Level 2 cuts out the foundation of your authenticity.

Being stuck at Level 2 is definitely a lot better than being trapped in Level 1. At least you are doing something. People caught in Level 1 often have a problem honouring their commitments to anyone or anything.

Sometimes people can be stuck at Level 2 for years without even knowing it. I recently talked with a friend who is a driven Achiever but is stuck at Level 2. He is extremely successful, with several businesses and a large staff. As we talked he divulged that he was very stressed because one of his businesses had been losing money for years. In fact, the profits of his other business were being used to prop it up.

"So why haven't you sold it?" I asked.

He replied that the business that was losing money had the highest profile and he worried that he would lose prestige in his community. He also admitted that it was his least favourite business and he was sick of it constantly draining him, personally and financially. As we talked, he realised that he had based his commitment on wanting to look good rather than living life on his own terms. By the end of the conversation he had made a commitment to sell the business.

This person was travelling at a very high speed. He was more or less heading in the right direction, but he was stuck on a side road he didn't really want to take.

I have seen people who stay focussed only on external commitment pay a high toll emotionally, physically and often financially. That is why I have always been a little wary of high octane motivation seminars that focus on just "doing something", anything. It may be a good initial step, however it is crucial that you also follow your unique, authentic path.

Being motivated to continue down the road of Level 2 is ultimately not in your best interest. It can be very draining and can lead to making commitments that you really didn't want to make in the first place. Essentially, at Level 2, the judge and jury of your performance is external. It is based on what other people think, and because of this, your level of success will always be erratic. If there is no one around who you have to perform for, then there is a really good chance you will just cruise along without pushing your own edge.

I remember an experience I had of being caught in Level 2 when I started going out with my wife. On one of our first outings together, I picked her up in a sports car that I owned at the time. As she was about to get in the car I asked her if she would like to take the wheel. She looked at me with a mischievous smile, climbed into the driver's seat and proceeded to drive the car in a way that I had never seen before. I felt like I was in the car with a Grand Prix racer as she fanged around corners with a relaxed confidence. Later I found out that her father was a racing car driver and had shown her the ropes.

At the time, my male ego was twisted a little out of shape. A few nights later I thought I better show her that I also had the skills of Schumaker. Now normally when I drive I am a bit of a cruiser. Cars for me have always been vehicles to get from point A to B. On this particular night, however, I looked like I was auditioning for a James Bond movie. I came around one particular corner well within the speed limit but definitely over steering. I suddenly realised I wasn't going to make it no matter how cool I looked. I ended up putting a dent in my ego and the car. Essentially, I was committing to a level of driving that was based not on my own expectations but on what I thought someone else expected of me. In fact, in this case my future wife had no expectations at all. It was all my imagination.

In reality, when you operate with external commitment, you are not usually operating in ways that others want, but rather in ways you *think* they want. It takes a lot of energy to figure out what you believe is the correct standard others expect of you. Then it takes a whole lot more energy to comply with those perceived expectations. Ideally, you would not be affected by what others think of you.

External commitment can also become an issue for people on an inner journey. Choosing to go for personal and spiritual change because someone else thinks it's a good idea has its problems.

I remember a middle-aged man called John in one of my seminars. He was participating in everything we were doing but looking very uncomfortable.

During one of the breaks I sidled alongside him and asked, "So John, how are you doing?"

In a very flat, uncomfortable tone he replied, "Not bad".

I just shook my head in silence to give him an opportunity to keep talking.

"Actually", he said, "I'm finding it a bit tough. You see, it's my wife's idea that I come along. She reckons I've got something to learn and she's probably right."

The end of his sentence trailed off as he looked thoughtfully at his shoes.

I looked at him and said, "Listen John, you need to figure out if you really want to be here. The only way you can ever really change is if *you* decide to change. It's up to you. Don't do it for anyone in this room or anyone else in the world for that matter. Do it for yourself, because that's the only way it will effectively work. In fact, I won't think any less of you if you decide to leave."

He looked up in surprise. I think he was waiting to be coerced into "going for it". What I was doing though was giving him the opportunity of jumping to the next level of commitment and choosing for himself, to drive the car to his own destination rather than someone else's. Eventually that is exactly what he did. He left the seminar, took some time out to think about what he wanted to do for himself, and then came back of his own volition. From that point on, he really began to change.

3: TOWARDS YOUR POTENTIAL—INTERNAL COMMITMENT

Someone who is highly evolved in the realm of the Achiever, has internal commitment, the third level of commitment. At Level 3 you are your own judge and jury. This is a level of commitment where you operate at your highest level of performance. It is based on the satisfaction of knowing that you went to your own personal limit and did what you really wanted to do.

To return to our journey analogy, at Level 3, you have packed your bag, said sorry to your friend who asked you to go to the movies, and headed off to the destination of your choice, that place by the lake. It is your unique journey.

Shifting to Level 3 gives you a tremendous sense of freedom and independence. You are free to decide what you want to do. Rather than trying to live up to others' expectations, you're setting your own goal posts. When you operate from internal commitment, you always know when you have been giving it your best. At Level 2, operating from external commitment, there is always the possibility that you can delude yourself. You are looking out into the world, hoping to gain the approval of others. However, at Level 3 you know if you're being true to yourself. You are looking within. Your attention is inside and you automatically know at what level you are playing the game.

Operating from Level 3 is very freeing. You are playing life on your own terms. It takes a lot less energy to live up to your own standards than to live up to the expectations of the whole world.

Sometimes people believe that they can go to someone and get "fixed". However, deep personal and spiritual change only happens when you choose it. I do not believe anyone can "fix" anything for you. People such as myself can only act as a catalyst for change, an aid or an ally in your journey, much like a coach to an individual or a team. Some people I have worked with thank me for creating a "new" them. However, it isn't me that is doing the changing, it is their inner commitment. They are creating themselves. The *real* person has emerged.

The pitfalls of acting with external rather than internal commitment are particularly evident in intimate relationships. Someone who operates from Level 2 can put on a tremendous show in the beginning of a new relationship. They may be charming, do exactly what you want, and fulfil all your expectations. In reality, this person is controlling themselves to please you, behaving just as you want them to. As the relationship progresses, this becomes unsustainable, and they will inevitably revert back to who they really are, which may be a completely different person to the one you were attracted to in the first place.

However, if you find yourself attracted to someone who is operating with internal commitment, what you see is simply what you get. When it comes to relationships you know what you are getting into right from the start.

Does operating with internal commitment mean that you do not honour commitments made with other people? No. You are more likely to honour these commitments because you want to, rather than have to. The Achiever who is operating from Level 3, completes their external commitments because of the drive generated by their internal commitment. Their internal commitment is to excel and be their best.

Essentially, moving to Level 3 is about becoming more of your own person. What often happens for people as they move from Level 2 to Level 3 is they fear that they will be disliked or abandoned. Initially it is a bold and courageous step. As someone moves to Level 3, they attract others of the same type and create even deeper and more sustainable friendships. As they grow in their own inner strength, they attract others that match them.

4: FROM THE ORDINARY TO THE EXTRAORDINARY—TOTALITY

> *"The only way to discover the limits of the possible is to go beyond them into the impossible."*
>
> ARTHUR C. CLARKE

The fourth level of commitment is called "totality". Totality is where the mission becomes more important than the person on the mission. It is the realm where you go way beyond what you considered possible. Everything extraneous vanishes from your field of vision and nothing else matters but achieving your intention. When you are at Level 4, you are in the car, on the way to the destination of your choice, with the turbo chargers fully engaged. It is the ultimate level of commitment for the Achiever. Whether it is in your career, your relationship, or your spiritual life, totality has the power to let you soar with the eagles.

Operating at Level 4 gives you the ability to be a tower of strength because you are giving life your best shot. Your rock-solid and unwavering focus makes you dependable and reliable. You emanate a sense of certainty. There is a sense of totality about you because that is what you are being – total in your endeavours.

Totality brings you out of the ordinary into the extraordinary. Level 3 people who have internal commitment are great achievers. Level 4 people who have mastered totality are extraordinary Achievers. Muhammad Ali was such a person.

In 1974, Ali was scheduled to fight George Foreman, the heavyweight champion of the world. Almost every sports journalist in the world believed that Ali could not win against the awesome power of Foreman. Most people were so certain that Ali was doomed that, as he stepped towards the ring, a television commentator remarked that the world may be watching Ali's last bout. In that first round, Ali threw everything at Foreman without seeming to make a dent. The months of anticipation had finally arrived and Ali realised that Foreman was much stronger and younger than himself.

Norman Mailer, who was covering the event, said that the end of that first round was the only time he had ever seen fear in Ali's eyes. Then, in a single minute before the next round, a powerful transformation came over Ali that would change the course of the entire fight.

Mailer said it was as if Ali looked right into the eyes of his maker and began nodding his head, as if saying to himself, "Now's the time, you have got to do this, you are going to do this." Diving down into the very depths of himself, Ali surfaced with the certainty of his own conviction.

By the end of the eighth round, Ali had achieved the impossible, and Foreman was beaten. Ali was the new champion and had cemented a place in history as one of the greatest sporting achievers of all time.

When asked by a reporter what he would have done if he wasn't a boxer, Ali's reply showed he was a man operating with totality. He replied, "Well I would have been the world's greatest at whatever I did. If I was a garbage man, I would be the world's greatest garbage man!"

Totality doesn't just cover the sporting arena. It is valid for every area of your life. And it is not just well known people who achieve totality. Bob and Evelyn were one of the most inspirational couples I ever met. They were so total in their relationship that you always felt there was no place in the world they would rather be than with each other. They were first loves and had been committed totally to each other for over forty years. Everybody in their neighbourhood loved them and found their marriage inspirational.

Highly accomplished achievers have a single-minded totality which gives them the ability to harness huge amounts of energy and channel it into a project. For example, Doris Haddock, affectionately known as Granny D, felt so passionate about showing people that life wasn't over for the elderly, that at eighty-nine years of age she walked 3,200 miles across the United States. Defying popular opinion, she exceeded even her own limits and inspired countless thousands.

THE FAST TRACK TO INNER TRANSFORMATION

"Vision isn't enough unless combined with venture. It's not enough to stare up the steps unless we also step up the stairs"

VANCE HAVNER

When someone approaches their spiritual quest with a sense of totality there is no height they cannot scale. I have seen people who approach their own development with such tenacity that they are transformed beyond their expectations. They undergo changes that are so profound that their facial features literally alter. Old burdens fall from their shoulders and a new light shines in their eyes.

At the end of one of my more advanced seminars, I was interested in finding out who had experienced profound change. I explained the concept to the participants. "Profound change is where you feel that the person you are now is not the same person that started this event. The kind of change where you know that from now on you will experience a quantum change in your ability to be successful, powerful, joyful and spiritually present."

I asked those who had experienced profound change to stand together in a group. After this group had assembled I then addressed the entire group.

"I want you to ask yourself the following question and be completely honest without in any way judging yourself. How many of you participated during the entire event in a state of complete totality, the kind of state where you participated with utter conviction from your own free will?"

Every person in the group that had experienced profound change raised their hand. They were the only ones. None of the others had hands raised.

Shortly after this, a man who had not raised his hand approached me with a clenched jaw, and a serious demeanour.

"I'm pretty upset," he said. "I wasn't part of the group that experienced quantum change and I'm pretty upset with myself. It has also been one of the biggest realisations of my life. I've been coasting along and I know deep down in my gut that I'm capable of so much more."

That one realisation altered the course of his life. He left the event with a burning commitment to maximise his potential.

If you approach your inner journey in the state of totality you open the doors for miracles to occur. I have received letters from spouses who have said that the person who returned from the seminar and walked through the front door was the person they had always dreamed of loving.

Many years ago, I attended a gathering in which Indigenous people were teaching some of their culture to a group of about sixty from around the world. A very quiet Native American elder caught my attention. He was solidly built, had deep, coal black eyes and walked with a deliberate step, as if he was always aware of the earth beneath his feet. One day, he announced to the whole group that he would be conducting a ceremony the next day at 3 a.m. and everyone was welcome.

The next morning, as I walked through the quiet winter darkness, pulling my coat as close to me as possible, I wondered how many others would be at the fireplace on the little knoll that was our designated meeting place. As I approached the fire, the only point of light in a sea of darkness, there were three other people waiting. We were the only ones that made it that morning.

The next two mornings at 3 a.m. the same group assembled. During both of these meetings, very little was said. Up until this point, our guide had spoken in vague generalities with occasional touches of deep wisdom. Often as he spoke he would look at the fire or out into the darkness as if talking to some unseen visitors. He was tolerant but also reserved and distant with us.

On the fourth morning when we assembled at the knoll, it was an entirely different story. He was right there with us. Suddenly the flood gates opened, and over a period of weeks we were taught a ceremony in precise detail that had come down through his family for four hundred years. Why had he waited? He was wanting to find out who was really committed. Indigenous people have wisely learned that it takes a high level of commitment to be able to utilise the mysterious power that is in their ancient practices.

HOW TO EXPERIENCE BEING EXTRAORDINARY

STEP 1: 100% ATTENTION

There are two steps in achieving totality. The first is to summon all your attention. Let's imagine that your attention or focus was divided into units, which I will call "attention units." The total number of these units is 100, which is your total capacity for focus and attention.

If you are engaged in a project, the first step is to bring all of your 100 units of attention into the project.

Take something very simple, like having breakfast. The average person eats breakfast with probably anywhere between 30 and 70 attention units. What if for just one day you were to bring all 100 units to the table. Imagine what the food would taste like and how the conversation would flow. It would probably make your breakfast a much more heightened experience. Similarly, people who experience car crashes, report a heightened awareness of the entire incident. At that moment all 100 units are at their command, focussed on what is happening in the moment.

The average person saves their 100 units for extraordinary occasions. *The extraordinary person summons all of their attention into average events and makes them extraordinary.* Someone who is committed to being extraordinary and living in a state of totality has the ability to make the most out of life. They are able to draw the right situations to themselves to lead them to their goal. They can do this because totality allows them to vibrate, so to speak, at a higher tone or frequency. When you are in this state you create magic – the ability to achieve the seemingly impossible.

When I was in the real estate business, I was asked to look at a big development that had been on the market for eight months without a single unit being sold. The owners were desperate. If nothing was sold soon, it would put them in an awkward financial position.

I decided to take over the project only after everyone on my team agreed that it was not only possible, but certain that we would sell every single unit. The whole team was committed to the project and approached it in a quiet state of ferocious totality. It was an honour and a privilege just to be around such people. After we made this commitment, things began to fall into place. The right people showed up who loved the area and wanted to buy. Within six weeks the entire development was sold out. The owners could not believe the turnaround.

Over the years I have told this story quite a few times. The most commonly asked question is about the strategies we used. My answer is that the strategies were secondary to the commitment. In other words, the strategies were only effective because the commitment was there in the first place. If you fully commit, the correct strategies will spring forth. They will naturally unfold. Two people with different beliefs can use exactly the same strategy and get completely different results. It is their directed thought that is the powerful force.

Just as commitment can take you to a state of totality, commitment to not achieving can also be self-realising. In this way, I had a very clear example of how you can use the principle of thought to *thwart* what you want. Recently I was talking to a young, troubled woman who had been on welfare for many years. She told me that her philosophy in life was to never get her hopes up about anything. That way she could never be disappointed. Without skipping a beat, she then complained that no opportunities ever seemed to come her way.

This person was essentially a prisoner of her own belief system. I could see and feel that she had so little self-confidence or positive energy that she was unable to draw the right opportunities to herself. As I watched her, I observed that she was unwilling to bring even a small percentage of her attention to anything in life. For this woman to take the first steps on the road to totality, she needed to bring all of herself into her projects and goals.

STEP 2: CLOSING BACK DOORS

The second step to achieving totality is to eliminate your back doors. A back door is a thought or action that sabotages your intended outcome. It is an escape hatch that you consciously or unconsciously know runs counter to what you want. When you commit to something and remove the back doors, you make an irrevocable decision. It is a goal from which you cannot escape.

Let's say you have a goal to make more money. At the same time, you are not prepared to take any risks or work any harder. Not working harder and being unwilling to take risks are two back doors that stop you really going for your intended outcome. Imagine someone saying to you, "I'd like to be more assertive as long as no one becomes upset". You could see straight away that they were not really total in their commitment. They had left themselves a back door.

I once worked with a shy, retiring woman who stated that she had never had a successful relationship. Her goal was to have a deeply fulfiling, long term relationship. As we talked she also realised that she wanted to be free without having to commit to anyone. She was able to see that this was her back door. It was her way of not being fully committed to her outcome. On realising this she was able to make the conscious decision to close the back door and become more committed to what she wanted.

A good example of closing back doors can be seen in a group I worked with who were high achievers wanting to stretch themselves even further. One of the participants decided that his goal was to lose 28 kilos in weight. He was successful in many areas of his life, but when it came to shedding weight he always seemed to falter.

As he looked around the room he said, "I have been on a lot of weight loss programs but none of them have ever really worked. This time I am going to lose all 28 kilos because if I don't lose it in the next six months I will donate $50,000 to charity."

There wasn't a sound in the room. Everybody knew that he was 100 percent committed to his goal. In one fell swoop he eliminated his back doors. Every time he thought about going near the refrigerator, he reminded himself of what would happen to his bank balance. Needless to say he completed his goal.

When you combine eliminating your back doors with bringing all of your attention to a project, you attain the totality of the Achiever.

READY. SET. CHARGE!

THE SECOND GREAT QUALITY OF THE ACHIEVER IS ACTION

Ready. Set. Charge! Actually, forget the "ready, set". For the Achiever it's just charge! Action is paradise to the Achiever. They love storming the ramparts of their latest mission. To master the second great quality of the Achiever, you need to become action oriented.

HOW TO CREATE EXTRAORDINARY OPPORTUNITIES

How do you become more action oriented? The answer lies in what I refer to as "windows."

Imagine you are playing a computer video game. As you travel through the game, you have the ability to click on certain characters or locations. This allows you to open different windows that take you to entirely new and amazing worlds. Each window opens a new opportunity for fortune and glory.

Well that is what life is. Life is like a 360 degree, virtual reality computer game. There are always countless windows or opportunities appearing in your life, and each one has the ability to take you on a whole new adventure. All you have to do is dive through the window. We have all experienced these moments. Perhaps your window came when you mustered up the courage to ask someone out on a date. This may have led to a new life direction.

We all have windows in our lives. It isn't about finding more windows, it is about being aware of the ones that are right in front of you. Achievers dive through them.

Sporting legends have made careers out of jumping through windows. When a professional tennis player hits the ball they are looking to place it in a very precise window. The fact that the ball is coming towards them, forces them to take action. They have to take the best possible opportunity when hitting the ball back. Life is the same, it is always coming at you. What may seem like a chance encounter, could be an amazing opportunity.

Sometimes a window will beckon you for ages, other times it is a matter of seconds. You never know how long a window is going to stay open. Life is always moving and eventually that window will close, or you will pass it by. The key to taking action is to develop a window-leaping mind set. Just start training yourself to grab opportunities that are right in front of you.

Mary Ellen Sheets was on her own, with two teenage sons, no money and a rusted, old pickup behind the house. She looked long and hard at the pickup and decided to act. She designed an ad promoting "Two men and a truck". Along with her sons, she put the old pickup into action and created a company by the same name. Her business grew into a vast transportation company grossing $40 million a year, with offices in seventeen states across the U.S. Mary Ellen Sheets was someone who recognised the old truck as representing a window she could jump through.

Often people wait for their one big lucky break. The key to getting that one big break is to take all the small breaks that lead up to it. To seize your occasional big opportunity you need to step through all the small windows first. This creates the mind set of the Achiever.

Many successful film stars are well-developed window-leapers. For example, Jodie Foster spent years in bit parts as a child before finally starring in her first big role in *Taxi Driver*. Paul Hogan was a rigger on the Sydney Harbour Bridge when he went on a television talent show. After his appearance, he was picked up for a five minute weekly segment on one of the networks. This led to his own show and eventually to the film Crocodile Dundee. All of this came from one window of a talent show.

The more windows you dive through, the more seem to present themselves to you. It is important to get in motion and start taking even the smallest of opportunities. Sometimes you just have to take action, you have to take a risk.

If you are someone who is shy, try initiating a conversation with the person next to you. If you are frightened of asking for that promotion, go ahead and do it anyway. Start stretching and building those risk muscles.

Inertia is just a habit. You can make diving through windows a habit too. The more you learn to take risks and develop this habit the more it becomes ingrained as a natural response.

GETTING WHAT YOU WANT

Often a window will open because you have set an intention that you want something to happen.

I remember many years ago setting an intention that I wanted to increase my personal power. Not long afterwards I found myself in a situation which challenged me to do just that.

I had an opportunity to do business with an extremely powerful person. I was organising a special journey with several colleagues and we managed to attract an extremely powerful and sought-after man to be the guide. At a crucial moment in the lead up to the journey taking place, the guide threatened to pull out if we did not do everything the way he wanted. This included a financial arrangement which amounted to embezzlement.

I remember walking around thinking, "I don't understand. This really felt like an amazing opportunity and now everything has turned sour." Then I remembered my original intention. I suddenly realised that I had a wonderful opportunity to increase my personal power.

Although at the time it was very unpleasant, I stood up to the man in question and called his bluff. Even though I was putting the whole event in jeopardy, I was determined not to compromise myself or my principles. I saw the situation as an opportunity to grow.

In the end, the guide backed down and the event was a great success.

Often when you look back on an experience that seemed horrible at the time, you see the blessing in it.

SETTING YOUR INTENTION

"If you trap the moment before it's ripe,
the tears of repentance you'll certainly wipe:
But if once you let the ripe moment go
You can never wipe off the tears of woe."

William Blake

Sometimes when you set an intention for what you want it might take a long time for that window to open. One of my windows took eleven years.

When I was twelve, my passion for surfing was just beginning to grow. One day, I was in a movie theatre watching the latest surfing film. As the film rolled into a segment on big wave surfing, I was on the edge of my seat, transfixed, as the big wave heroes of the day tackled those mountains of water. I remember thinking, "One day I really want to do that". I also remember doubting that I ever could.

Eleven years later, I woke up one morning and heard the growling rumble of a huge sea. Local veterans were calling it the biggest clean swell they had ever seen. People had taken the day off work and were crowding the beaches just to get a look at this awesome spectacle of nature.

None of my surfboards were big enough for those waves, so I went down to the shed and pulled out a dusty old red surf ski (like a canoe) that I hadn't surfed for years. As I walked to the beach the headland was crowded with hundreds of people. There were surfers hanging out of trees, gazing from rocks. No one was out in the water. As I paddled out I remember that time as if it was yesterday. My heart was pounding so loudly it felt like a jackhammer in my chest. I had enough adrenaline coursing through me to light up a small town.

The media have popularised the concept of human beings beating the elements of nature. Nothing could be further from the truth. It is like an ant climbing to the top of an elephant and claiming victory over the elephant. I was feeling extremely insignificant out there alone in that organised mayhem.

As I paddled out to sea, these gigantic liquid bombs exploded down the reef. The waves were so big you could place a truck inside the barrel, the tubing part of the wave. The air itself was three times more alive and charged than any big waterfall I have stood next to. It is a strange thing that when the ocean gets this big everything looks like it is moving in slow motion.

I picked off a few of the smaller monsters before paddling out the back. By then, I was nearly half a mile out to sea. There had been a lull for nearly ten minutes, an eerie silence. As I looked out I saw a dark looming shadow blank out the horizon. It was one of the biggest waves of the day. I started paddling furiously out to sea. Through my peripheral vision I could see a lot of the crew on the headland pointing at the wave. I didn't need any warning though, the last thing I wanted was to get buried under this wave.

As the wave started dragging on the ocean floor it became more vertical. I paddled up what seemed an endless wall of water. The ski felt like a match stick underneath me. Except for a few stray thoughts, I was fully in the here and now, focused on getting over the top of this behemoth. To my right the wave was already pitching, producing an awesome barrelling cavern.

I could never say what made me do it. Perhaps it was instinct or a small boys intention all those years ago in a movie theatre. As I neared the top, I realised this wave was surfable. I quickly turned the ski 180 degrees and started paddling down the face of the wave. The wave picked me up and I looked straight down a watery cliff. I hurtled down completely vertical, lying fully extended, my back compressed against the ski to stop it from nose-diving. I knew that if I didn't pull off a turn it was all going to be over when the nose hit the base of the wave.

I lent way over and the ski arced around and up onto the face of the wave. I was travelling across the wave now. It was so big I couldn't see the top and the bottom of the wave at the same time through my peripheral vision. The speed was phenomenal. Behind me I could hear the wave crashing, echoing like cannon fire. I surfed the wave to the very end and as I came over the top, the crowd on the headland start waving and cheering. I punched my fist into the air, totally exhilarated and hooting with unmitigated joy. A childhood dream had come true.

The interesting thing is that ever since then, I have never seen a swell quite like that one. If I hadn't gone out that day, deep down I would have regretted it. That is the price you pay if you don't leap through windows.

THE ACHIEVER'S TOOLKIT

HOW TO BECOME ACTION ORIENTED

How do you achieve drive and become more action oriented? Your performance will be affected if you have too many commitments and if the quality of them is poor. You need to find out if you have overcommitted yourself or if you have committed to things that you aren't really passionate about. The first step is to check the number and type of commitments you currently have. Have you ever been having a shower when someone turns on all the taps in the house? What happens to the water pressure? Suddenly the shower loses all its power. When you make too many commitments it is like turning on every tap in the house. You run the risk of dissipating your power.

DISCOVERING YOUR PRIMARY OBJECTIVE

> *"Things that matter most must never be at the mercy of things which matter least."*
>
> GOETHE

Generally speaking, there are six key areas in your life that you can commit to. These are:

Spiritual life
Relationship
Family life
Career
Recreation and hobbies
Contribution to humanity

To make sure you are not over-committing yourself, prioritise which is the most important area for you in your life. Place a number, with a pen (or mentally) next to the most important area, all the way through to the least important. It is crucial as you do this for you to eliminate the word *should*. When you prioritise the list be true to yourself. Be honest. Don't write what you think you *should* write, write what you really know inside to be true.

Getting this list in order helps you to become clear about the priorities in your life. If you try to do a host of other things outside these areas you will look like a juggler who has too many balls in the air. Eventually one of them has to fall.

Once you get clear on what are the most important key areas in your life, the next thing is to look within each of these areas. If you have too many commitments in one area, all the other areas will be affected. For example, if you have nineteen balls in the air at work and the stress is mounting, this will start to affect your family life and inner life. You can only be effective if you limit the number of commitments you have within each of these areas. Too many, and you run the risk of losing momentum in all of the key areas.

One effective way of determining what are the most important commitments in your life is getting clear on your desired outcomes.

BECOMING CLEAR ABOUT WHAT YOU WANT

Your desired outcomes, or what you want, will determine the quality of commitments you make, which will in turn effect your success. You are making commitments all the time. Sitting in front of the television at midnight and downing a tub of chocolate ice-cream is an action that first starts as a commitment. Like all commitments it begins as a desire, then, as you leap out of the chair to the refrigerator, it becomes a commitment. The only problem is that it is probably not a quality commitment. It is not a commitment that empowers you. It leads to an action that you might regret.

Accomplished Achievers are very clear on which goals they wish to achieve and which commitments they need to make to achieve these goals. They are aware that to be successful they have to delete anything that is unnecessary or a distraction to their desired outcome.

THE SECRET OF OUTCOMES

When I was training myself to increase and develop my Achiever I had a small sign next to my bed adhered on the wall right near my pillow. It was the last thing I saw before I slept and the first thing I saw in the morning. There were only four words on that little sign.

> "WHAT IS MY OUTCOME?"

Those four words referred to the desired outcome I wished to create in the world. For several months I measured all my tasks by those four words. If I was preparing to go shopping I asked myself, "What is my outcome?" It was amazing how many shopping trips were suddenly scrapped because I realised that I didn't need to go shopping that day, I could wait for the next. I would go to my office and every task would be measured by those four words.

I realised that in the realm of the Achiever there are only results. I didn't want to go to work to take up time, I wanted to produce. That was my desired outcome, to produce results. Suddenly I realised how many phone calls didn't need to be made, and how many extraneous endeavours I was pursuing that did not lead me to my outcome. My income rose and the hours I worked radically decreased.

I am convinced that many people work long hours simply because they think that they *should*, to mitigate their guilt. They think that unless they are putting in long hours, they aren't achieving anything. If your desired outcome is to climb to the top of a mountain, you have two options. You can call a committee meeting, plan the route and the supplies you will need, talk to others who have climbed the mountain and start the journey. Or you could just climb the mountain. If you are very clear that your desired outcome is to get to the top of the mountain, then you will take the second option. If, however, your outcome is to feel busy and hard working, then you will probably go with the first option.

To develop your Achiever try this exercise. For one month, measure everything you do by asking yourself, "What is my outcome?"

If you are going for a run, ask yourself "What is my outcome?" If the answer is to get fit, that will dictate the pace. If the answer is to get some fresh air and have fun, then it will be a different type of run.

If you are going to meditate, is your outcome to sit there for one hour or is it to still your thoughts and achieve inner peace? Personally, just sitting for an hour is a waste of my time, but achieving inner peace sounds good to me.

Do you get the picture? Why are you doing what you are doing?

When I am really busy and get a chance to spend time with my family, I ask myself those four magic words. My answer is usually, "Well instead of just hanging out and passing time, what I would really like is an experience where we all feel fulfiled." I am seeking an interaction full of laughter and in-depth conversation. That is my desired outcome.

The same question is also invaluable when dealing with obstacles that come up in your life. If you are faced with a problem, rather than letting the problem control you and becoming obsessed with how bad things could get, look for an outcome you want, a solution, and stay focussed on it.

If you try this exercise for a month, your whole life will develop another characteristic of the Achiever – efficiency.

TURNING THE TOUGH ROAD INTO THE EASY ROAD

> *"Two roads diverged in a wood and I—*
> *I took the one less travelled by.*
> *And that has made all the difference"*
>
> ROBERT FROST

From the Achiever's point of view there are only two roads in life. The first road is the path of discipline and persistence. The second road is the path of procrastination and distraction. For all but the highly developed Achiever, the first looks like the tough road and the second feels like the easy road.

If you have a project that needs to be accomplished in three weeks and you put it off to the last minute, you take the easy road. However, the ironic thing is that it eventually turns into the tough road when you start feeling stressed and working overtime to complete the project by the deadline. If you discipline yourself and start the project early, it may feel like you are taking the tough road, but this eventually leads to the easy road. It becomes less stressful and your life feels more balanced.

People who spend all their money on instant gratification are taking the easy road. Those who learn to save and invest take the tough road in the beginning, but end up reaping the rewards of the easy road later.

If you go along with the crowd, do what you are supposed to do and never take risks or go for your dreams, you may think you are taking the easy road. Eventually though, the easy road turns into the tough road. I often hear elderly people say it is not the mistakes in their life they regret, it is the opportunities and dreams they never went for.

Taking the easy road leads to the tough road. This applies to every endeavour. If you don't awaken your elements, life may start on the easy road but it will eventually turn into the tough road when you don't get what you want in life. If you awaken your elements it may be a little tough in the beginning, but in the end it will feel easy as you achieve a quintessential life.

Probably one of the most common areas in which these two roads appear is in our health. Let's say you decide to take the easy road. Minimal effort is your maxim. Your recipe is a lot of junk food mixed with a lot of coffee and alcohol, all combined with the athletic prowess of Homer Simpson. Everything goes fairly well for a while. "Hey, no sweat, literally, an extra twenty or thirty pounds never hurt anyone."

However, as Newton said, "For every action there is an equal and opposite reaction." That old easy road slowly turns into the hard road. The body just doesn't seem to have the get up and go like it used to, and you start developing aches and pains. Of course if you spend a few more years travelling that easy road then the road might get harder and harder (and so may your arteries!).

Now, let's say one morning you wake up and your Achiever grabs you by the throat and says, "Enough is enough, You're getting in shape!" At first it might be tough, changing your diet, eating healthy foods, puffing around the block and going to that yoga class. Gradually though, you start to feel better, your energy picks up and you're looking and feeling great. If you stay with it long enough, the good diet and exercise becomes a habit and something you enjoy. Voila! The tough road becomes the easy road.

If you lose your health through misfortune that's one thing. If you forfeit it through years of taking the easy road, that's another.

Most of life is about choosing these two roads. Eventually choosing one road will lead to the other. This doesn't only apply to your health, but also to your career and relationships. It might be easy to get into a habit of just watching television with your loved ones at night. However, if you don't allow the time for intimate conversation, eventually it turns into the tough road, as family members become more distant. If you want to have more peace of mind and harmony in your life, you have to take the tough road in the beginning. Without the fire of the Achiever willing you to go down the tough road for a while, it is difficult to ever attain the easy road.

Sometimes you know which road to take, but linger on the easy road by trying to delay your decision.

As I was writing this chapter, the phone rang. It was a friend who was facing a difficult decision. After listening to his dilemma I said, "Why don't you intend that within 36 hours, you will know the answer to your question – which direction you need to take. Actually," I continued, "you only need five minutes. You may believe that you need a day and a half, but you really know the answer right now, don't you?"

My friend laughed and agreed.

If you are not fully in your Achiever, you will limit and delay what is in the interests of your highest evolution by always choosing the easy road. The developed Achiever will take the tough road because they know it will turn into the easy road.

OVERCOMING OBSTACLES

> *"Obstacles are those frightful things you see when you take your eyes off your goal"*
>
> HANAH MORE

It is important to realise that you are always going to make mistakes. There will always be setbacks. It is how quickly you recognise and correct those mistakes that makes the difference. If you have ever sailed a boat you would know that you are always correcting the course. You cannot set a course and stay on it. You must allow for the tides, wind shifts and other factors. You may be heading for your goal, which you can see straight ahead. However, you will rarely get there by travelling in a straight line. That is like life. Occasionally something goes exactly to plan, just as the wind may blow you straight on course. Most of the time, however, you need to keep adjusting the course to get what you want.

If you want to achieve great things, the key is to develop a mind set that picks you up off the floor after a setback as quickly as possible. What makes this easier is knowing and accepting that these setbacks are simply challenges. Life will constantly present you with challenges.

The Achiever has a very simple outlook on life that can be boiled down to a simple directive: "Want something? Go get it." To "get it" the Achiever has a formula for success.

THE ACHIEVER'S FORMULA FOR SUCCESS

1. Make a commitment
2. Take action
3. Deal with setbacks
4. Re-commit
5. Take action

You make a commitment, take action, deal with any problems you may run into, pick yourself up, recommit and start all over again. The key is to persevere, to just keep going.

This formula applies to every field of endeavour whether it is spiritual or material. For example, you commit to meditating and stilling you mind. Out of the blue a stray thought enters your mind and you re-commit once more to the process.

Most great works have been achieved through this formula. The award-winning novelist Elizabeth Jolley was rejected by nine publishers before one agreed to publish her first book. The Beatles were rejected by ten recording studios before Capitol signed them up. R.H. Macy failed seven times before his store became a huge success in New York.

Success is rarely an overnight phenomenon. The key is to embrace challenges and setbacks as a natural part of life. Wanting life to be perfect and free of challenges is not only unrealistic, but also creates inner tension and discontent.

I have often heard people say that if they could just make more money, then life would be perfect and they wouldn't have any more problems. If it isn't money, then maybe it's a new car or relationship that is the missing key to perfection.

Someone who is evolved in the Achiever knows that life will always be challenging. It is this knowledge that takes the sting out of setbacks. This understanding creates a tremendous freedom because you no longer see challenges as bad or horrible, you perceive them as the natural order of life. Once you know this, life becomes an extraordinary adventure.

Most people see their life as a series of benefits and inconveniences. A lot of the pain that humans experience is often created by trying to avoid some disaster happening. Have you ever noticed that calamities are often easier to deal with than the apprehension about them occurring? These are experiences designed to help us grow. Until the day you check out, you will face challenges. If you can fully accept this fact you will experience a momentous shift in the way you feel and perceive life. Try saying to yourself with excitement and conviction, "From here on in, life will present me with challenges". The Achiever embraces this viewpoint and draws strength from it.

TRAITS THAT SELF-SABOTAGE

THE ONE-DIMENSIONAL ACHIEVER

If your only developed aspect is the Achiever, you can fall prey to becoming stuck in a rut. You may only see the "straight ahead and charge" approach, not realising there might be numerous options to get what you want. This can lead to exhaustion and to overriding you intuition.

If your only developed aspect is the Achiever, all you ever need to know about your shortcomings will be revealed in observing a fly.

Have you ever seen a fly trapped inside a room trying desperately to escape through a closed window? The little dude or dudette gets a full head of steam and, driven by the desired outcome of escape, batters their little noggin into the glass.

There is no doubt they are clear on their desired outcome – freedom. Intention they have in abundance, but success? The scoreboard reads: Window – 1000; fly – nil.

People whose only developed aspect is the Achiever can be as manic as the fly trying to escape. Just watch them when they first start a project. They can drive people around them to distraction.

You probably also know a few achievers who seem magnetised to the brick walls of life. They keep racing down the road, dressed in their red and blue superman or superwoman outfit, only to smash into an obstacle at high speed. Sure, they do have a few wins as not all roads lead to brick walls, and they know about perseverance, but their red and blue outfits hide many bruises and scars.

Any fly (or human for that matter) who had a highly developed Sage would perceive the glass. Their wisdom would dictate that this glass was impenetrable. The Sage is the one that says, "Hey fly, I love your speed and intention but it would be a good idea to turn left now". But this Achiever does not believe in inner voices - CRASH, again.

I've never talked to a fly in this state, but it looks to me that they are not having much fun. The Poet would say, "Hey, lets chill out for a minute. We'll take a break, check out the sights and come back to the problem with some renewed energy."

The Visionary Leader would say, "Hey, wake up. Forget that window. That's not your path. Look over there – there's a window that's open." Ever seen a fly do this? Just metres away there's an escape but they can't see it.

Of course, our Spirit would simply say, "What's all the fuss? Surely you don't think you're really just a fly?"

Thinking about the fly reminds me of someone I met many years ago. I wouldn't have been more than fourteen years old, but this one small encounter burned its way into my brain.

I was coming home from school when I walked into a shop at a railway station to buy something to eat. I started chatting with the owner of this tiny shop, talking about my day. Then he said with an air of resignation and despair, "Another day gone, another day closer to the grave." He looked so tired when he said it, like the kind of fly who has realised he's going to die behind that window without ever getting through. This man was old before his time. He was a good person who was a one-dimensional Achiever. He worked really long and hard hours and was courteous to his customers, but he was doing something that produced very little love and a meagre reward.

THE EXTRAORDINARY ACHIEVER

The consummate Achiever is someone who has reached the highest pinnacle in the realm of the Achiever. This state is attained when you go beyond personal survival. You know when you have touched the absolute heights of the Achiever when you have transcended your fear of death, committing to a vision with such fierce intensity that nothing else matters except the achievement of the goal. Sometimes, as in the case of Stuart Diver, it is the fight for life itself that is the goal. At this point you go to your true edge. You have crossed the line and your mission becomes more important than your safety and security. This pinnacle is the most sublime feeling for an Achiever. People such as Martin Luther King and Mother Teresa arrived at this pinnacle. Their personal mission became bigger than themselves.

BEYOND FEAR

Tina Strobos was a young medical student in Holland in the late 1930s with everything to live for. She put it all on the line as an active member of the Dutch underground. Tina and her mother provided food, shelter and false identity papers to many Jews, thus saving their lives. They would hide the displaced and hunted people behind false panels in the house. When the Gestapo searched the premises, they knew it would be death for all of them if they were discovered.

Bram Pais owes his life to Tina's courage. Pais was a brilliant physicist who went on to work with some of the leading scientists in the world after the war. He had been the last Jewish student to receive a doctorate before the Nazis banned Jews from higher education. Pais hid for years in tiny rooms with false walls. He subsisted on simple food and kept himself fit by doing push-ups and other exercise. One day, towards the end of the war, he was betrayed. The SS arrested him and he awaited certain death. Tina Strobos, risking everything, approached an SS official and convinced him to release the brilliant young physicist.

Most people who never go for their dreams have a fear for survival.

A friend of mine who is very wealthy often remarks that the reason most people aren't wealthy is because they are not willing to go broke. It is their fear of losing safety and security. When you transcend this fear for personal survival you feel a tremendous sense of freedom. It doesn't mean that you harbour some kind of death wish. On the contrary, it allows you to really live because you don't feel constrained.

An example of transcending personal comfort is the inner spiritual journey. For most people who first begin this journey, discovering the concept of inner freedom is an exciting prospect. As you travel a little further, however, you begin to realise that to be truly spiritually aware you have to move beyond your comfort zone, not physically, but emotionally and spiritually. You have to give up the mask you wear. To let your inner diamond radiate, you have to peel away the layers of your false self. It is a form of death with a rebirth to a higher level of awareness. At this stage of the journey a fear often arises that if you keep going you will lose your sense of self. In reality though, you end up finding a stronger sense of self.

When someone crosses the line between security and risking all, they become trustworthy. Why? Because you know where they stand. You may not agree with them or even perhaps like them, but you do know where they stand. Someone who has really embraced the Achiever and stepped across the line is very easy to "figure out". There is no middle ground. They are going for it.

"It's never too late to be what we might have been"

George Eliot

For many years, a small group of people had been asking me to do a course that would be completely outrageous -an incredible adventure that would stretch them way beyond their current limits. They had all attended many of my seminars and wanted to take part in an event where they could experience truly crossing the line.

We were scheduled to helicopter into one of the most beautiful and dangerous environments I have ever encountered: the glaciers and mountains of southern New Zealand. There the weather can change from sunshine to snowstorms in less than twenty minutes. The chopper pilots who fly there, and who have flown around the world, rank it as one of the most dangerous flying environments they have encountered. Apart from the deep snow and jagged mountains, there are glaciers with hundreds of crevasses. These crevasses are often well over a hundred feet deep and covered with a thin snow bridge. To the naked eye it looks like you are stepping onto flat snow. In reality, it is an invitation to the last six seconds of your life.

The interesting thing about extreme elements of nature is that they magnify everything. In the mountains or out at sea, if someone in the group is not committed it affects not only their survival but everyone's. In fact, the great paradox of commitment is that not being committed increases your risk. Wavering in the middle of the road is much more dangerous than going to either side. There is nothing wrong with committing to *not* do something, for example, I take one look at ice hockey and say, "No way". It is the middle ground that is dangerous.

There were three of us leading the mountaineering expedition: myself; Matt, a well-known mountaineer; and Paul, a doctor with extensive knowledge in remote medical rescue who was also an expert Himalayan climber.

On day one of the expedition, everyone was excited. The group had flown in the night before, and now we were all gathered, a host of eager faces, in a small room scattered with back-packs, piles of ropes, crampons and other mountaineering gear. The place looked like an adventure sports store. Everyone had been briefed well before the event as to the hazardous nature of our little sojourn. We had all been in training for several months.

During the meeting the conversation turned to the actual procedure we would be following when in the mountains. We would be travelling in small teams to maximise safety when the helicopters dropped us at the head of the glacier. As we talked we could feel the sense of exuberance in the room, and with two days to go before we would finally get on the glacier, everyone was quite relaxed. That was until our medico, Paul, rose to speak.

Paul has a very quiet, unassuming manner that cuts straight to the point. He said, "I need to handle one important logistical requirement. In case anyone does end up at the bottom of a glacier, we need to find out if you want your body left there or brought back home."

Talk about a reality check! Everyone was instantly alert and present. It was decision time. The message was clear to each person. It was time to cross the line. Those who had been feigning a macho air suddenly became humble. What had been a "seminar", suddenly became a life-affecting commitment.

A few days later some of the members of the group talked about that moment of decision. They realised that they had been playing it safe in so many areas of their life. They had been holding back in their relationships, careers and their inner journey. It was a powerful time of learning for everyone.

THE POET

"To see a world in a grain of sand and a Heaven in a wild flower, hold infinity in the palm of your hand and eternity in an hour."

William Blake

A JOURNEY TO A NEW WORLD

I am used to planning my teaching schedule a year in advance, so I know exactly where my destination will be when I get on a plane. However, last year we decided to do something completely different. Annie and I usually plan our vacations together but this time we hit on an extraordinary idea. We decided that for our next three week holiday, I would not make a single plan or strategy. All I knew was that the destination was Europe.

My wife, who was born in Finland, said, "I'll show you the real Europe."

"Ah, this will be different," I thought to myself. "Time to let go of control." I felt an adventure coming on.

To add spice to the deal I agreed to be a passive passenger, to make no decisions and to offer no suggestions. I could feel myself relax and expand just thinking about it.

I turned up at the airport, suitcase in hand, feeling tremendously excited. Here I was a seasoned world traveller, and it was as though I'd never been to an airport before. I felt like a kid and I couldn't stop smiling. I wondered what was in store for me.

All airports have the same feeling, as if you are in a transition room, a room full of people on the way to somewhere. As we approached the counter, I saw the sign—Zurich.

"Ah Switzerland." I felt a pure joy as the first piece of the puzzle dropped into place. A tingling sense of adventure was coursing through my body.

It was a couple of hours after arriving in Zurich when it really hit me. We came around a corner and there in front of me was a scene from a Tolkein fairy tale. I gasped in wonder and tears filled my eyes as I looked across the river to the striking old town of Berne. The 1000 year old town, rose solidly up from the river bank.

At its base, majestic ramparts like a fortress seemed to speak of another time. One minute, a modern world, the next an ancient one. I hadn't expected it and was completely taken by surprise. No wonder the world is such a place of amazement to little children. It is still fresh and new.

We travelled on through winding mountainous roads and the clear sweet air of the Alps where an endless vista of solitary peaks stretch out to the horizon, through tiny rural villages where farmers worked the land by hand, all the way to the opulence and wealth of the Riviera where diamonds and luxury cars competed for attention.

Every time we landed in a location, I had no idea where we were headed to next. My urge to plan went out the window as all my attention was channelled into one day at a time. I remember looking out from the hotel in Monaco at the sleek white yachts on the still blue sea, feeling utterly carefree and at peace with the world.

We cruised on through the sun-drenched towns sandwiched between the azure waters of the Mediterranean and the rising green hills. The sensual holiday ambience of the coast was wonderful. Every day the sky was cloudless.

We crossed the Italian border and arrived at an old fortress town situated on a craggy hill in Tuscany. I spent days inside the walled town, wandering through 800 year old back alleys and lane ways. I remember walking down one of these twisting darkened passageways finding the most exquisite detailed carving, hidden from prying eyes. I gazed at it wondering who the forgotten artist was who had carved in such precise relief this hidden work of art. How many centuries ago had they toiled? Did this mark the wall of some once noble family, now forgotten? If this carving had been on a building where I came from, where "historic" is measured by a single century, it would have been one of the gems of the city.

After one of the most amazing weeks of my life we were sitting in the Piazza of Venice, one of the most romantic places in the world. The Piazza, which is about the size of two football fields, is surrounded by the most beautiful statuesque gothic and renaissance buildings. Napoleon called it the drawing room of Europe. Not a single car could be seen – all transport in the city is through the twisting watery canals.

That night the city fulfiled its other namesake – "La Serenissima," the most serene. It was a warm, still summer's night. The sun had just set and a full moon hung above the horizon like a perfect yellow orb. Behind our table an orchestra of violins and pianos produced that stylish passion of which the Italians are masters. Women selling roses competed for space amongst the flocks of swirling pigeons. As I looked into the eyes of this very beautiful woman across the table I could feel the presence of Venice all around me. It was the atmosphere of love and romance. I felt the enchantment of life.

THE POET'S BLUEPRINT

"Water is fluid, soft and yielding. But water will wear away rock, which is rigid and cannot yield."

LAO TSU

Probably no city in the world represents the Poet as much as Venice. It is built on one hundred and seventeen small islands and water is the life blood of the city. It has a myriad of canals providing transport and beauty.

Water, like the Poet, is the great nourisher. Without water a beautiful garden dries up, withers and eventually dies. We humans are the same. Without the watery Poet we become dry and lifeless. If you are overworked and burned out then you need an injection of the Poet.

To understand this element, watch a leaf in a bubbling stream. The leaf's journey down the stream does not resemble the straight flight of the Achiever. Whereas the energy of the Achiever is like an arrow flying through the air, the Poet flows like a spiralling circle. The Poet is more concerned with the process than the destination. The leaf is unpredictable in its travels, visiting one side of the bank before getting caught in a small eddy. Just when you think that it will be caught there forever, the water suddenly takes it on another adventure to the other shore.

Although it may seem gentle, don't underestimate the power of this stream. Eventually it will wear down the hardest of rocks, creating lush fertile valleys. The Poet, through its most powerful agent, love, has the ability to ease your cares and make your life beautiful. Like the stream it can wear down mountains of stress and tension. The high point of the Poet is love. You cannot really put words together to define love; that state of grace is something to be felt and experienced.

Poets, like water, are fluid. They are spontaneous, loving and in a constant state of renewal. Poets experience beauty, being in the moment, romance and joy. They are optimistic, bubbly and hopeful. The Poet has their heart open to the world. The Achiever believes that happiness will come when they get to a goal, the Poet experiences happiness irrespective of where they are. When you have both your Achiever and your Poet fully awakened, you can head towards your goal and still enjoy the process.

Poets value love and harmony above all else. They abhor conflict and shrink from aggression. They are great romantics with wild flights of imagination, and in their ideal world everyone is happy and gets along. They want to see a world that is a paradise, full of pleasure. They long for surroundings that are joyful and serene. Their nature is one of great sensitivity. A kind word can lift them to the heights of inspiration and a harsh word can cut them to the quick. As a result, they are always on the lookout for environments that can soothe their soul and uplift their senses.

They love inspirational conversation, seeing it as a vehicle for connecting with other people. It is a way they can establish friendship, love and a deep connection.

THE GREATEST GIFT: AN OPEN HEART

THE FIRST GREAT QUALITY OF THE POET IS *HAVING AN OPEN HEART*

"It is only with the heart that one can see rightly;
what is essential is invisible to the eye."

ANTIONE DE SAINT-EXUPERY

One of the great qualities of the Poet is an open heart. What is it that produces an open loving heart? The answer lies within two different streams of love: self-love and compassion.

THE FIRST STREAM OF LOVE: SELF-LOVE

"To love oneself is the beginning of a lifelong romance."

OSCAR WILDE

The first stream of love is the one you direct to yourself. If you are overworked and tired it is very difficult for you to feel love for yourself or anyone else. The first stream is about taking care of yourself and giving to yourself. This starts by scheduling enough time to eat well, sleep well and exercise well. These are your basic building blocks. It is also very important to schedule time to nurture yourself.

When I am on a hectic schedule in some new city, one of the first things I do is find out who are the best masseurs in town. Scheduling time for a good massage is a great gift you can give to yourself.

There are so many different ways you can nurture yourself. Take a walk in nature, go out to a fine restaurant, join a yoga class or buy yourself a present. You are your own best asset and you need to look after yourself. I have talked to people who feel they can't give to themselves because they see it as selfish. However, if you can't nurture yourself, you can't nurture anyone else with a full heart.

THE SECOND STREAM OF LOVE: COMPASSION

The second stream of love is the one you direct towards others. Love in action is called compassion. Compassion is where you give of yourself to help others, such as in the following story.

Dr Russell Conwell was someone who knew the meaning of compassion. One day, as he was walking outside his small church in Philadelphia, he saw an unkempt little girl dressed in ragged clothes, sobbing in distress. On enquiring what the problem was she told him that she had been refused admittance to Sunday school because there wasn't enough room. Dr. Conwell took her by the hand and escorted her inside and found a place for her to sit. The little girl was so deeply touched that she went to the poor tenement building that was her home and told her parents about the kind man who had helped her.

Two years later the little girl passed away and her parents not knowing who to turn to, sought out Dr Conwell to help with the funeral arrangements. As they were moving her frail little body, they found a dirty old purse that looked like it had been pulled from the garbage heap. Inside the purse was a total of fifty-seven cents and a scribbled note in the little girl's handwriting: "This is to help build the little church bigger so more people can go to Sunday school."

Robert Conwell read the note with tears running down his face. He was determined to make this little girl's dream a reality. He set about raising the large sum of money necessary and the donations began to pour in. He was still short of sufficient funds when fate took a strange turn. A newspaper printed the story, and a realtor was so touched by it that he offered Dr Conwell the land for the total sum of fifty-seven cents.

In a room adjoining the Sunday school in Philadelphia, is a portrait of Dr Conwell and the little girl who inspired a dream.

That one little act of compassion, when a kind person took a little girl by the hand, led to an event bigger than either of them could have imagined. With an act of compassion, you never know where it will lead. A kind word might be a lifesaver to someone in distress.

EMPATHETIC LISTENING

You don't have to look very far to give compassion. It can start with the people closest to you – your family and friends. One of the simplest ways of improving relationships is to use empathetic listening. This is the kind of listening where you are fully present and attentive to what is being said, where you have a genuine desire to truly comprehend what you are being told.

If you have ever been in love, you know what empathetic listening is. You can probably remember being fascinated by what your lover thought, felt and experienced. You wanted to know what made them tick, what they believed in and what their dreams were. As time goes by it can be easy to think that you "know" someone and so you slowly forget to listen to them. However, people can often be undergoing change right in front of your eyes. If you don't recognise this change, they can feel hurt and misunderstood.

Empathetic listening is like having a large sign flashing above your head that reads, "I care." It is a magnet to people. I remember a brilliant observation someone once made to me: "interesting people are interested". Ambrose Bierce said the same thing in a humorous way when he defined an egotist as "a person more interested in himself than me."

So many people are starving for affection and love in our society.

People are silently crying out to talk and be heard.

A story about Mother Teresa clearly illustrates this need for love and affection. She reflected that even though people in her Calcutta home for the dying were in great poverty, they were surrounded by loving family members and even the sick ones usually had a smile on their face. She contrasted this to a nursing home she visited for the elderly in a western country. Everyone in the home had good food, televisions and all the necessary comforts. As she walked around she noticed that no one was smiling and every one was looking towards the door. She turned to the sister and asked, "Why do these people who have every comfort, not smile? Why are they looking toward the door?"

The sister said to her, "This is the way it is nearly every day. They are hoping that a loved one will come and visit them. They are hurt because they are forgotten."

We are often inspired by stories of people working for great humanitarian causes, however you can start practising compassion in your own home. Start by giving to someone right in front of you. In the beginning you might feel you are doing all the giving and they are doing all the receiving. As you go along on your path, however, you discover that by spreading your love, it is you who is on the receiving end. Compassion opens your heart, and there is no greater gift you can give yourself than an open heart.

THE DOORWAY TO THE SPIRITUAL PATH

An open heart is the doorway to the spiritual path.

A friend of mine once told me that the greatest spiritual journey is only twelve inches long. It is the journey from the head to the heart. In Chinese the words "heart" and "mind" have the same root. In fact some schools of Chinese medicine believe that "the heart rules the mind", meaning that when your heart is troubled your mind is not centred and peaceful.

A spiritual path without love is not a path, it is just a belief system. Love takes you beyond the belief and gives you the experience of the

Divine Force. It is the foundation of spirituality all over the world. Over the centuries, Christian mystics have described love as the fruit of their prayers. The Dalai Lama claims, "My true religion is kindness." The Indian holy man Ramakrisna once encouraged a woman who wanted to find the love of God, to first start by loving her family. A loving, open heart brings joy to yourself and those around you.

Having an open heart is not something you need to develop, rather it is something you need to reclaim. We all possessed an open heart when we were little. It is something we are all born with and is one of the most endearing qualities of small children. Jesus Christ said, "Except ye be converted and become as little children, ye shall not enter the kingdom of heaven."

You can learn to reclaim the love and joy you once possessed as a child. One of the keys to reclaiming this state is to find out why it disappeared in the first place. The answer to that lies in the word *trust*.

CREATING EASE IN YOUR LIFE

> *"He who can no longer pause to wonder and stand rapt in awe is as good as dead."*
>
> EINSTEIN

If you watch someone who has an open heart, you will find that they have a high degree of trust – trust in people and trust that everything will work out for them. Trust creates a tremendous sense of ease in your life. If you observe someone who does not have the quality of trust, you will find that they lack joy, laughter, innocence and fun – all qualities of an open heart.

Years ago a very successful man came to see me who complained that life was totally dry and joyless. He was a scientist and talked about how his studies had led him to believe that there was no life after death. In fact he felt that life itself was a meaningless state of affairs that could be explained by scientific, rational processes.

I looked at him and said, "As a scientist, you would know that quantum physics is anything but rational. The discoveries that have been made in that field prove that the world is a mysterious place and disprove many rational scientific theories. Einstein himself discovered some of his principles by imagining himself riding on the end of a beam of light."

He replied, "I know all that and I have studied quantum physics. But to be effective in that field you have to take a leap of faith and I just can't take that leap."

That leap of faith was a leap of trust and he just couldn't do it.

When we look at great minds such as Buckminster Fuller or Einstein we find not only the wisdom of the Sage but the childlike innocence of the Poet. They see the world as a place of wonder and constant learning.

When you have the trust of the Poet it allows you to see the world with fresh eyes. When you combine the childlike trust of the Poet with the discrimination of the Sage, your trust matures. You learn that the most important thing about trust is to trust your intuition about situations and people.

I knew a man who had several relationships in a row that became very sour. He made a decision that he was never going to be hurt like that again. He closed his heart to any possibility of ever having a fulfiling relationship. Subsequently, all the joy in his life dried up and vanished. When his life became so dry that it was painful, he decided to risk having a relationship again. This time, however, he decided to use his discrimination.

When he looked back on his past relationships he saw a destructive pattern that had spelt doom to all of them. Using his discrimination and intuition he was able to find someone who was completely different from his previous partners. The new relationship blossomed and he is now happily married with three children.

If you use the discrimination of the Sage, you can learn from the experience, but you need the open-heartedness of the Poet to embrace the lesson. If you have had a bad experience in the past, it does not mean that your future experiences will be negative. The key is to keep your heart open and use your discrimination.

TRUSTING YOURSELF

"As soon as you trust yourself, you will know how to live"

GOETHE

The highest level of trust is when you begin to realise that there is very little that can hurt you. When you have a deep trust in your own abilities to extricate yourself from difficulties, and when you have an implicit trust in the Divine Force, you begin to realise that ultimately you can find some good in everything that happens to you. When I look back on my life there have been some challenging times. However, with hindsight, I have learnt something positive from every one of them. Even if I had the power, there is not a single experience I would take away. They were all experiences that helped me grow, evolve and learn.

When I was not long out of school I travelled in Africa. I secured a job that supplied educational products to children. The company paid monthly, and just before I was about to receive my cheque, the company closed its doors and left all the employees high and dry.

I remember at the time sitting on my bed with a total of about forty cents to my name. It wasn't enough money to buy lunch. I felt as if my world had caved in. Here I was, thousands of miles from home, with no money for food or rent. Even if I went out and got another job it would be a week or a month before they paid me.

As "luck" would have it, a friend of mine showed up with some cartoon posters that they were successfully selling on the street. I grabbed a whole bunch of posters and talked my way into the biggest shopping centre in Africa at that time. I convinced the management to let me into the central forecourt, the premier location.

I proposed that I would let all the kids colour in my posters while their parents went shopping, if the management would let me sell my posters to the public. They loved the idea and decided not to charge me rent. It was a few weeks before Christmas and I made more money than I would ever have made in the previous job.

Better than the money was the education I received. It taught me the basic principles of business and how to think on my feet. What at first appeared a tragedy became a blessing. I have always found that as one door shuts, another door opens.

When you know and trust that everything is for your higher good, it creates a quiet joy and serenity. The key is to look at a situation and see it from a higher perspective. Perhaps there is something in that situation you need to learn so you can continue to grow.

JOYFUL SPONTANEITY

"As youth fades and time brings changes, we may change many of our present opinions. So let us refrain from setting ourselves up as judge of the highest matters."

PLATO

One of the keys to establishing trust and having an open heart is to learn how to be more in the moment. In a sense, being in the moment is one of the attributes of trust, letting the future unfold in its own way and own time. When you are in the moment, you open the door to joy and spontaneity.

There are two areas of the Poet's life that force you to be in the moment. If you have ever been in love or had a really good belly laugh, all that exists is the here and now. You are not thinking about the past or worrying about the future, you are totally in the moment. In fact it is not possible to do either of these things *unless* you are in the moment.

I remember one day running along the beach. It was a very beautiful day with hardly a cloud in the sky. As I was running, I was thinking about my first meeting of the day. I was hoping to get into the office early so I could clear up some paperwork. In my mind I started to go through exactly how I should fill out the paperwork. After I did the paperwork, I started to write the advertisement for this week's paper.

Suddenly I stopped in my tracks. It was a beautiful day and I wasn't even noticing. I thought to myself, "you've got to be kidding".

I have met people who are so consumed by the past or the future that if you were to ask them at the end of their life-span "How was your life?", their only honest answer would be, "I don't know, I was rarely there".

I once heard it said that the present is a gift. That's why it is called the present. Our entire existence boils down to this moment, then this moment, then this moment. The Poet knows that the key to happiness is to be in the moment

BALANCE

Let's look at the concept of being in the moment. What I would like you to do is place an "X" on the scale above as to where you see yourself. If in most of your waking moments you are doing things and performing actions you would mark the scale like this.

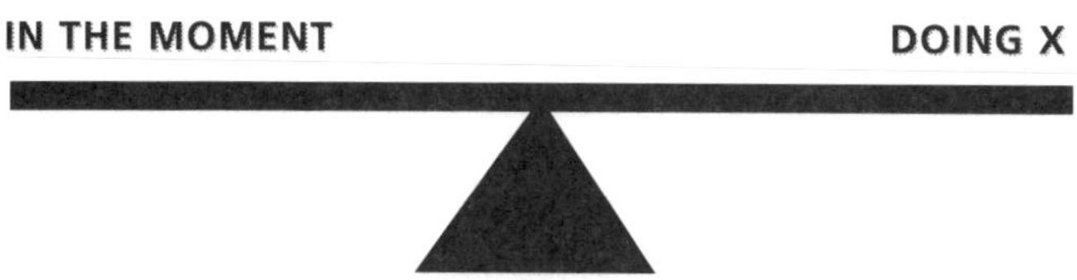

If you are someone who just loves hanging out, without ever having a plan, then your X would be at the other end of the scale, above "In the Moment."

If you were someone who was very balanced between "In the

Moment" and "Doing" then your X would be in the middle of the scale.

Most Achievers will be on the "Doing" side. Most Poets will be on the "In the Moment" side, cruising in the present, singing "Don't worry, be happy."

If your X landed on "In the moment", you are probably someone who experiences a lot of joy but perhaps doesn't get a lot done. If your X landed on "Doing", you probably experience the satisfaction of being productive. However, satisfaction and joy are not the same thing. Satisfaction is nice, but joy is amazing.

When the Achiever and the Poet form an alliance something wonderful happens. You are totally present in the moment whilst performing actions.

There was once, in one of my seminars, the Managing Director of a very large company. Her name was Michelle. Michelle's "X" was so far on the "Doing" side that it was almost off the page. Nothing much existed for her outside of work. She had sacrificed a lot to be the head of a major company, but felt burned out. From the moment she woke in the morning to the moment her head hit the pillow at night, her brain was on the go. Her partner was also a constant doer and the marriage was suffering. She felt they only had time for brief snatches of conversation over hurried cups of coffee.

Michelle wanted to be successful but also have a life. When I explained to her about the different elements, her eyes widened. She became extremely excited because she could see what the problem was. Her Poet had basically been buried under her constant drive. As she began using many of the principles outlined in this book, her Poet awakened and she became more spontaneous, loving and generous. People at work began to comment. Everybody appreciated her light touch and less serious demeanour.

A lot of people like Michelle are concerned that if they embrace the Poet they will lose their drive and ambition. You can awaken the Poet and maintain your other strong elements. In fact this synergy of all the elements can actually enhance your success.

THE SECRET TO HAPPINESS: MASTERING THE INNER WORLD

One of the keys to being in the moment and establishing a sense of trust is mastering your inner world.

There are two worlds constantly operating for every individual. The inner world and the outer world.

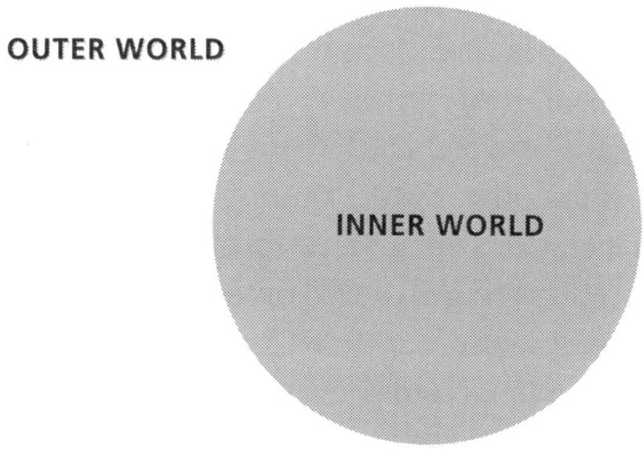

Look at the circle above and imagine that everything on the outside of this circle represents your external world. It is the events that happen around you and to you, such as going to work, meeting friends, etc. It is all the experiences and interactions of your life.

The inside of the circle is how you emotionally respond to the events that happen in your external world. Many people believe that their happiness is determined by what events occur in their external world. The real key to happiness and equanimity is not so much what occurs in your outer circle, but what you feel in your inner circle. It is the ability to take responsibility for what you feel rather than seeing what you feel as being determined by external events.

There was a study undertaken where people were asked to find a ten cent piece that had been hidden. Those who found the ten cents responded with a much higher level of happiness than those who didn't. When you think about the difference a dime can make, it's pretty ridiculous.

Let's say you are in your car on the way to an important meeting and you suddenly hit bumper-to-bumper traffic. This is an event that is taking place in your outer world. As you sit there you begin to feel a growing frustration.

"This is outrageous. What the hell is going on up there. I wonder when this will be fixed. God, why is this happening to me, I just don't need this right now."

As a result of the traffic jam in your outer world, a response happens in your inner world. The response in this case produces feelings of frustration. The message is clear: "this traffic is making me feel bad."

If you assume a position of complete responsibility, you realise that the traffic can't make you feel bad. If you decide it is the traffic's fault, you are saying, "I am powerless, I am not responsible for what I feel." You are handing over your ability to choose what you feel. Essentially what you are saying is, "my outer world has complete domination over my inner world".

When you allow outside circumstances to dictate how you feel, you make yourself infinitely smaller and less powerful than you really are. When you choose to operate more from your inner world, your confidence and ability to handle problems will soar.

DON'T WAIT TO BE HAPPY

"If you are distressed by anything external, the pain is not due to the thing itself,

but to your estimate of it; and this you have the power to revoke at any moment."

MARCUS AURELIUS

Victor Frankl was someone who had a horrendous outer world. Frankl fell under the iron boot of the Nazi purge of the Jews. His wife and parents were ruthlessly killed and he was repeatedly tortured in one of the death camps. Frankl discovered that even though his entire outer world had been demolished, there was one area of his life that his captors could not touch. That area was inside himself. He realised that internally he was still free to decide what he would think and feel. Even though the guards made his external world a living hell, they could not enter his internal world. He was the one that had the lock and key to that domain. He decided to be happy despite what was happening around him. Victor Frankl succeeded and became an inspiration to his cell mates and later to the world.

The truth is that you always have a choice with your responses. You choose your inner world at every given moment.

If something occurs in your outer circle that really upsets you, the natural thing to do is to release that emotion rather than store it inside. When you think about it though, how many things are really worth getting upset about. You are the one who has the power to make yourself happy. Your circumstances do not control you, you control your inner circle and your feelings. You can make it a wonderful life.

I know multimillionaires who are very happy. I also know people who never seem to be satisfied, no matter how much they have. There is a litany of rock stars and famous people who had everything, but traded it all for the needle or bottle.

There is nothing wrong with having money and beautiful things in life. The Poet loves to surround themselves with beauty. However, you delude yourself when you say that you will only be happy when you have those things. You can be happy right now. It is a choice. In fact, you can be happy with very little as I discovered when I visited a very remote island in the Indonesian archipelago with a group of friends.

We had been travelling for days over some of the thousands of islands that make up Indonesia. We were "island hopping." We would drive all the way across one island, then put the cars on the archaic ferries, and move on to the next port. Each time we headed further away from civilisation. Finally we arrived at an island for which no tourist brochures existed and where white people rarely ventured.

There is something that takes place when I am far away from civilisation. Being in the natural environment with people who have not been ensnared by the western world allows me to remember what is really important in life. On the island time moved very slowly.

We had been on the road all day. In reality, calling the pot-holed dust bowl a road is a massive exaggeration. Everyone was hanging on to whatever they could grab as the car lurched out of another giant pot-hole. The bush surrounded us on all sides like something out of the African plains.

Finally I saw the village, a collection of thatch houses, up ahead. About the same time, the villagers heard the low pitch of the four wheel drives. No one owned a car in this village so they began to gather, curious as to who was visiting.

We drove closer, and a call went out as they saw our white faces. They were running towards the car, the shy ones in the back. God knows when they last saw people like us. Everyone mobbed the car, a sea of brilliant white teeth, set in happy brown faces.

Kim was the first one out of the car. He is a compassionate Rambo –a large wild man with a big heart. Kim towered over the huge mob of kids. He pulled a balloon out from his pocket, put it to his mouth and blew. All the kids were astounded as they watched the balloon expand. They had never seen this trick before, or, for that matter, a balloon. He threw the inflated balloon toward them and they went wild, laughing and jabbering a hundred miles an hour. All the adults were in on this now as well. Everybody was laughing and playing, watching as red, blue and green balloons bounced from hand to hand. Their laughter was so natural, playful and infectious that we all felt lighter.

As I looked around the village there were none of the conveniences that in our society we call necessities, yet these were some of the happiest people I had ever encountered. They genuinely cared for each other and were quick to share a smile. Their inner world was very rich.

It is worth keeping in mind that all of this joy in the village was over a bag of balloons that probably cost a dollar.

I have met so many people in our society who need a very large event in their outer world to produce a small shift of happiness in their inner world, such as those who believe that if only they had more money or got that promotion, they'd be happy.

If you are waiting for your external world to change before you can feel happy on the inside, you are giving your power away. Essentially you are saying "Hey, I'm not in command here. I am a leaf in the air being buffeted by the wind."

If you say to yourself that you can only be happy with a certain set of circumstances, then you give your power to those circumstances. If someone believes they can only be happy when they have a private jet and a ten bedroom house, then the jet and the house own them, the concept of the jet and the house contains the power. It is a subtle form of slavery and it is they who have enslaved themselves.

AWAKENING INNER JOY

THE SECOND GREAT QUALITY OF THE POET IS *APPRECIATION*

There is a plague that resides in the human heart and its name is judgement. We judge ourselves for what we are and what we are not. We think that if only we try harder maybe we could be acceptable to ourselves and others. Judging is exhausting, it robs us of our peace of mind. It is also ineffective. If it worked, we would all be enlightened by now. If you want to do yourself a big favour, just drop your self-judgement.

I have heard people ask, "If I stop judging things, then how will I know when I am off track?" There is a big difference between judgement and discrimination. Discrimination is when you realise a certain behaviour is not in your best interests. Judgement is when you believe you are bad or wrong for having that behaviour.

Let's say you realise that you need to develop more of the Poet in your life. Maybe you have been working very hard and neglecting your loved ones. You don't need to beat yourself up about it. You can just quietly correct the situation.

Judgement only makes correcting our behaviours more difficult. When you are in a state of judgement, you become more contracted and linear in your approach. It is like having a giant rudder on the bottom of the boat that runs from bow to stern. It makes the boat very difficult to turn. If you watch little children, or people that do not experience much self-judgement, you will find that they have a certain lightness about them. They don't take life too seriously. The more serious you are, the more difficult it can be to change. When you take yourself lightly, change can be simple because you are only dealing with the issue at hand, not all the additional baggage of those inner demons in your mind telling you how stupid you are.

I have found that the more someone judges themselves, the more prone they are to judging others.

A great example of non-judgement is a mother with a new-born. In their eyes the baby can do no wrong. To them everything is wonderful, every movement the baby makes is new. At the same time the mother is also experiencing a lack of self judgement. The mother has achieved one of the high points of the Poet, the state of appreciation.

Appreciation makes you more open and expansive. Appreciation is an elevated state that gives you tremendous peace of mind. Appreciation is accepting yourself and others the way you, and they, are.

THE JUDGEMENT EXERCISE

If you want to experience how pointless judgement can be, try the following exercise.

Go out into the garden and start talking to the plants out loud, or if you are the inhibited type, talk inside your mind. Start by having this conversation: "Hey, you're a good leaf, but you over there, you're not very good at all, in fact you're kind of irregular. You should be more rounded. Hey plant, you're too short, you should be taller and besides you're kind of pale, you'd be much nicer if you were a darker green. Wow, check out that blade of grass, you're the most pathetic blade in the lawn, can't you get it together!"

In doing this exercise you will probably notice that not only is judging plants silly, but it is also ineffective. Those plants don't change one bit. It is the same with people; you can judge them all you like but it usually won't change a thing.

When I look out the window at my rainforest garden the first thing I notice is how all the plants complement each other. There is no one "correct" plant. The tall green palms, with their bases wrapped in vines, are in harmony with every flower and leaf. The Poet appreciates all of nature, from the ancient tree to the budding flower.

If you think judging plants is pointless, isn't it just as ridiculous to judge humans? Is there some expert out there who has defined the ideal plant, the perfectly presented and socially conscious rhododendron? Then who is the expert that defines what other people should be doing?

The Poet appreciates the whole symphony of human life. When you open yourself to appreciate the different shades of humanity, you open yourself to joy. For Poets there is no right and wrong. They see people as fascinating and intriguing. Their range of friendships is wide and diverse.

A NEW WORLD OF EXPERIENCES

When someone becomes stuck in fixed behavioural patterns they lose their ability to have range. Range is the ability to appreciate many different people and experiences. When you lose your range, you confine yourself to a narrow bandwidth of experience.

Let's say you own a five speed manual car. Imagine saying to yourself, "Hey I don't like first gear. In fact I think first and second gears are pretty stupid and I'd rather not use them." You are instantly going to cut yourself off from one of life's common occurrences: moving up a steep hill from a standing start. It is the same with people and experiences. When you stop appreciating and start judging, you lose your range. You rob yourself of some of the incredible experiences in life's tapestry.

One of my favourite places in the world is on the eastern tip of Java. It is a wild jungle preserve. There are no roads or aeroplanes. The only way in is by boat. When I first used to travel to this wilderness the only habitation was a primitive camp on the edge of the forest overlooking the beach. The camp was a few straw thatched tree houses set on stilts. At night it was necessary to be off the ground and away from prowling leopards. It was very rare they would venture into the camp, but you would often see their footprints on the beach. As you sat looking out from the tree house at the waves breaking on the coral reef, you could imagine how Robinson Crusoe must have felt.

Approaching the beach by boat, you weave around the coral reef and see a thin ribbon of sand stretching along the coastline. The jungle begins just twenty yards from the waters edge; a steaming riot of deep green, an uneven carpet stretching in all directions away from the beach; an endless profusion of giant trees covered with a tangled web of vines. It goes on for as far as the eye can see. Monkeys play in the treetops. Down below, snakes as round as your arm move through the thick undergrowth.

After a few days the atmosphere starts to seep into your pores. It is wild, primal and restorative. You begin to feel what it was like before the advent of modern times, when the world was young. Self concern drops away. Sitting in the tree houses, listening to the surf and the strong smell of new life from the jungle, you feel alive, relaxed and wild in a very present kind of way.

In complete contrast, one of my other favourite places in the world is a very well-known, upmarket hotel. Every afternoon in the elegant coffee shop a small orchestra plays. The staff are extraordinary and genuinely friendly. The atmosphere is refined and beautiful. It is a sanctuary in a hectic busy world.

Now, which experience is "right", the jungle or the hotel? If you are a Poet, the answer is neither. They are both part of the tapestry of life.

Being able to experience the range of creation gives you tremendous flexibility. Just as there are five different gears on your car, you yourself also have different gears. Being able to open yourself to all your gears gives your life range and variation.

Sometimes I hear people say, "Well I'm just not that kind of person, I'm a regular, knock about type." Someone else may refer to themselves as only comfortable amongst society's elite. The truth is they do not have to be that way. They chose to be that way. Life is a choice. Poets understand and choose the whole tapestry. They are not content to exist in a little corner of the picture. For them the entire tapestry is their home. In their eyes and ears, every instrument in the orchestra has merit. Without each unique instrument the orchestra would be that much poorer. So it is with people.

If you are in a state of appreciation, you see the world as not only a place of discovery, but a place of learning. The world has many teachers, from people to nature. The quiet pond teaches you peace and introspection, and from the wild tempestuous storm you learn power and passion.

APPRECIATION AND THE PEACEFUL MIND

Appreciation creates a peaceful mind. Judgement destroys appreciation and your inner peace. Judgement enmeshes you with other people. Thoughts are not just contained within your brain, they travel. Have you ever had the thought that people were speaking about you and later had it confirmed? Have you ever been thinking of someone and not long afterwards, they phone you? When you focus your thoughts on a person, you place a telephone call on a thought level. The other person picks up the phone, whether they are consciously aware of it or not.

If you hold many judgments about people, it is like placing a lot of phone calls. Too many calls tie up your own telephone exchange. Just like an overloaded telephone exchange, you cease to function effectively. Your inner peace and your power disappears.

People who are quite evolved emanate a sense of peace and power. This is partially the result of not getting caught up in things that do not concern them. They recognise the futility of judgment and keep their phone lines free for important calls – calls from the Divine Force. The more you are at peace with yourself and others the more you are able to listen to your intuitive guiding force. This is the power of appreciation.

As you move along on your path, you realise that the only person who can truly judge yourself is you. It is your self-judgement that restrains you from being who you really are. Appreciation of yourself gives you the freedom to express who you are.

CREATING DEEP RELATIONSHIPS

"Between whom there is hearty truth, there is love"

HENRY DAVID THOREAU

One of the most beautiful gifts you can have in your life is a loving, deep relationship. A relationship that has depth is one where you can share the deepest part of yourself – all of your dreams and ideas, and your unique outlook on life. A deep relationship is an authentic relationship. It is a relationship where you share the real you.

People only reveal who they truly are when they feel safe. Safety is created by appreciation. Think about it for a minute. How safe do you feel to reveal who you really are when you are being judged? If you think you are being judged, you probably keep everything inside. When you extend appreciation to your partner it allows them to feel safe. They naturally begin to reveal who they are, thus adding to the depth of the relationship. *The following diagram explains how to have a love affair that lasts over time:*

THE LIFELONG LOVE CIRCUIT

The key to having and keeping a great relationship is to follow each step in the relationship cycle. Most relationships start at the top of the chart with Appreciation. In the beginning of the relationship there is

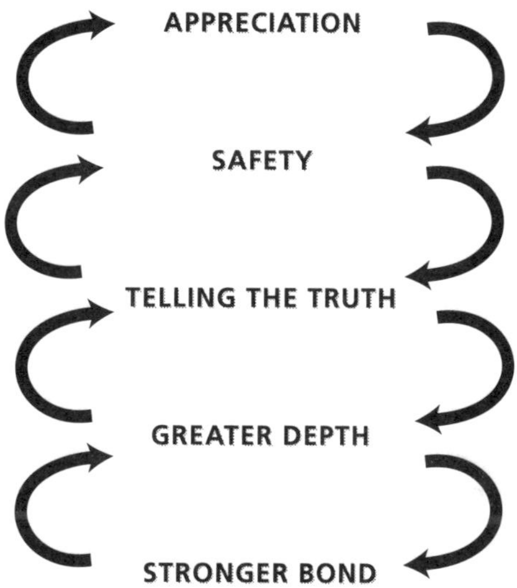

a tremendous amount of safety, lots of sharing and revealing the truth, which produces great depth and romance. After a while, two key areas in this chain can begin to break down. The first is appreciation and the second is safety. When people begin to lose appreciation and judge their partner, safety begins to break down. This can lead to withholding true feelings.

Let's say in the beginning of the relationship one person loves and appreciates their partner's spontaneity. Over time, as the relationship develops, they often feel impatient with the very trait they once appreciated. If there isn't a climate of safety within the relationship, then these feelings can remain unexpressed. Often both people worry that if they tell the truth, it might result in a look of disapproval or even a violent outburst. They begin to think, "Maybe it is safer not to say what I'm thinking and feeling." As they stop telling their inner thoughts and feelings, the communication becomes more shallow. If it keeps going along this path, the relationship can end up looking like one of those bland 1950's TV sitcoms: "How was your day, dear? Oh just fine."

If you don't reveal yourself at the deepest level there is a tendency to feel unfulfilled and misunderstood in the relationship. I may feel like something is missing. The relationship begins to lack the zing it used to have.

I remember a couple who came to a relationship seminar that my wife and I were holding. They had been married for many years but felt that the spark had gone from their union. As we explored this area they realised that they had been withholding a lot of secrets from each other. They were little things such as minor resentments and withheld inner feelings. One of the main reasons they no longer shared these feelings was that they were frightened of hurting the other person. However, when the truth goes out of a relationship, so does the passion.

As they began to open up and reveal their inner world their passion returned. It was wonderful to watch the sparkle in their eyes. These two people who were in their fifties looked like teenagers in love for the first time.

Appreciation doesn't just apply to your primary relationships, it is a necessary part of all your relationships. Being in a state of appreciation doesn't mean you have to condone actions that are harmful. It is about appreciating the person and pointing out what stands in the way of fulfiling their maximum potential. When my children were teenagers I always tried to hold this point of view and we managed to maintain a great relationship.

I remember a situation I was in where it was crucial to maintain a state of appreciation. I was giving a talk to some homeless teenagers. As I walked to the front of the stage and looked into their eyes, the first thought I had was, "sixteen going on thirty five." These kids were streetwise and sharp as a tack. They had to be, in order to survive on the street. Most of them had done a lot of drugs and some of them were at risk of becoming hardened criminals.

During the course of my talk I made it very clear that I thought drugs were a dead end, but I never judged them or lectured them. They had been lectured and told they were dead-beats all their lives. They didn't need to hear it again.

Over the course of my talk, the scepticism slowly began to give way and they started to open up. They revealed personal stories that they had probably never told before. Later I wondered whether I would have been any different if I had the upbringing they had?

You can never really know what someone has gone through, or what motivates them to do what they are doing now. All judgements do is limit the other person and limit yourself. If you look with a narrow perspective it may appear that the person is way off track. However, from a broader perspective it may be that some action you consider wrong or bad may be necessary for that person's evolution. Perhaps someone has to go way off track just to realise that they are not following their true purpose. Haven't we all done that at one time or another?

Many years ago a man called Neil, who ran a world-wide mining business, came to one of my seminars. The business was very profitable but did quite a lot of environmental harm. Neil was a very powerful Achiever who was also quite fixed on what his life was about. In his mind you looked out for yourself, your family and employees. Everyone else could look after themselves.

Quite often when you judge others, you are judging an aspect of that person that you yourself have, and as I examined Neil I saw a part of myself. I remembered there was a time when I just wanted to have a nice quiet life and look out for number one. Rather than tell Neil how wrong he was, I talked about my own life and how not having a purpose made me feel unfulfilled. I said that although I had been considered successful, there had been a part of me that didn't feel complete. After I finished speaking, Neil's eyes glazed over and he became very quiet and introspective. Somewhere inside him the story had touched a cord.

Several months later I saw him again. He told me that because of what he had realised in the seminar he had left his business. He'd been trying to convince himself for many years that everything was fine in his life. Deep down, though, he knew it wasn't. He had just embarked on a large scale project to help disadvantaged children. Because of his business expertise he was able get the project off the ground very quickly and was making a big difference in people's lives. The most striking difference, however, was in the way he looked. The "world weariness" had left him and he had a new lease on life. He said he hadn't felt so happy in years.

Being appreciative gives you your own inner freedom and grants permission for others to express who they really are.

DISCOVERING A WORLD OF WONDER

A very powerful way to awaken appreciation and increase your inner joy is to release a form of judgement called labelling. Labelling involves, quite simply, putting a label on any object or person.

When you are a child and you first look at nature, everything is a process of discovery. You are in a state of wonder. As you grow, you slowly, and at first imperceptibly, begin to label everything around you. You walk through the world and the running commentary goes, "That's a tree, that's a flower, that's a yellow flower."

The labels gradually become more specific. "That's a eucalyptus, that's a daisy." You begin to *know* what a daisy is, and over time the daisy only gets a cursory look because you subconsciously rationalise, "I've seen hundreds of daisies." The process of discovery ends right there. You now see the daisy in the context of your old knowledge about daisies. In fact, you don't really see the daisy at all. You see a concrete image from your past, superimposed over the daisy. You know what daisies are. After all, you are a daisy expert.

To recapture the appreciation of the Poet you have to forget what you know and be willing to discover what is before you now, with wonder and amazement.

WALKING WITH FRESH EYES

An exercise I highly recommend is one I have done with many people. I call it Walking with Fresh Eyes.

Go for a walk, preferably somewhere in nature. As you walk, don't label anything at all. If you are looking at a tree don't call it a tree. If your old conditioning comes up, then give it a completely different label. Use some gibberish to describe what you see. For example, if you are looking at a tree, say to yourself, "That's a very interesting hooden wat." If you see a flower, say to yourself, "Wow, I've never seen a ringwood before." This might sound odd, but it will break your old patterning. The whole idea is to see something as you've never seen it before. The key to this exercise is seeing things with fresh eyes.

People become bored with things because they "know" them. I have seen people who are hardened cynics return from these walks with a new-found wonder. Thomas Jefferson said, "There is not a sprig of grass that shoots uninteresting to me."

What determines whether something is beautiful or not? It is your perception of it. Someone sees the sun out and says it is a beautiful day. When it is raining, some say we are having bad weather. When you say that the weather is bad, you are labelling and judging. What is bad weather anyway?

I live very close to a long, beautiful beach. One of my favourite times to go walking is when it is raining. If you can get past the initial conditioning of, "Oh no I don't want to get wet", and really relax into being rained on, it is wonderful. Children love playing in puddles and the rain but after being told that they will "catch their death of cold" they begin to "grow up."

When you stop labelling, you start to see beauty instead of objects. Your vision becomes broader and you start to feel a sense of wonder in things you would never have even bothered looking at.

There is a beautiful Navajo prayer that sums this up:

"In beauty, I walk
To the direction of the rising sun
In beauty, I walk
To the direction travelling with the sun
In beauty, I walk
To the direction of the setting sun ....
All around me my land is beauty
In beauty, I walk"

When you have this attitude, every day is an adventure. You can go off and see the wonders of the world, but you can also sit and be absorbed in the coming and goings of a square metre of grass. If you look closely, there's a whole world in there just waiting to be appreciated.

As people grow older there is a tendency for the labelling and judgement to become more and more defined. As this takes hold in the mind, what people are willing to experience becomes less and less. They lose interest in exploring new areas and become fixed in small channels, better known as "ruts."

If ever I have a tendency to write-off a new form of music that my children love I always try to remind myself of when I was sixteen. I remember sitting with my grandfather when a rock band came on the television. His response was exactly the same with all of this music. He had one statement that covered everyone from The Beatles onward: "Long-haired gits." I asked him what was his favourite music when he was young?

He replied, "Ah, Bing Crosby. Now that was real music, beautiful music, not this long haired rubbish."

I then asked him, "So what did your parents think of Bing Crosby?" That stopped him in his tracks. With a slightly sheepish look he said, "Well they thought that was rubbish too."

The more you label and judge things around you as right and wrong, the further you move away from the Poet. Small children do not walk around judging things as right or wrong – that's why they are

Poets. Now don't misunderstand me, you *do* need discrimination to function in the world. The other elements give you discrimination. It would be extremely unwise, for example, to go to an intense negotiation with a hardball business person and only take your Poet. The key is balance. Without your Poet your life becomes dry and romance fades.

THE POET'S TOOLKIT

THE GATEWAY TO CONTENTMENT

How do you achieve a state of appreciation and an open heart? One of the most effective ways is through gratitude. Gratitude is one of the gateways to the Poet. By using gratitude your level of happiness can soar.

If you had a child that was always griping about everything they had, would you feel like giving them more? On the other hand, if a child thanked you and was grateful for what they had received, it would probably open your heart to give even more. When you are grateful for what you have, it is like offering a prayer to the Divine Force which allows more gifts to flow toward you.

I urge you to try the following exercise for ten days and observe the difference it makes. It only takes five minutes and has the power to change the way you view your whole existence. It not only changes your perspective but opens the floodgates for more to enter your life.

I find this exercise is best done when you first wake up or just before you go to bed at night. Buy a small notebook or journal and set aside five minutes every day. If you are particularly committed, try five minutes in the morning and five minutes in the evening.

Start a fresh page every session and write, "Today I give gratitude for . . ." across the top of the page. Then let the pen write.

There are two important aspects to this exercise. The first is to keep the pen moving. If nothing comes to you then just slowly make lines across the page. This way you will access a deeper part of yourself. Your words will be less contrived. Just wait until something pops into your brain – words or feelings. You might write, "Today I give gratitude for my spouse, my children, another day, my friends, my job, that great conversation I had with Mary," etc. If it has been a really rough day and the only thing you can honestly write is "Today I give gratitude that the day is over," then start with that.

The second important thing is to write down some things you are grateful to yourself for. You might write, "I'm grateful for my patience." or, "I'm grateful for not putting up with being taken for granted." or, "my compassion," etc. It is important to see yourself in a good light. This part of the process is vital. It allows you to be less judgmental and more appreciative of yourself.

I have often asked people, "Who treats you worse, your worst enemy or yourself?" Some people reply that they couldn't imagine a worse enemy than themselves. See if you can stretch yourself into recognising your good qualities and good points.

As you complete the exercise, write two simple words: "Thank you". See if you can genuinely mean it. Gratitude is a feeling or an energy rather than lip service. When you are genuinely grateful to the Divine Force for all its gifts, you open the floodgates for even more to enter your life. It truly is an awesome power. Not only that, your entire thinking changes. You start to see so-called negative experiences as learning experiences, they lose their sharp edges. The result is that you experience more equanimity and contentment in your life.

I can hear some people saying, "Oh great, if I get run over by a car on the day my insurance lapses, you want me to be grateful? You've gotta be kidding!"

Start off small and write things that are true for you. If you are not grateful for something, don't write it down. Remember to be authentic. It is not about being falsely nice.

HAVING EMOTIONAL BALANCE

Expressing yourself is another way of developing appreciation and an open-heart. There are two important forms of expression: artistic expression and emotional expression.

1. ARTISTIC EXPRESSION

Great painters, dancers, musicians and poets all have one thing in common. They are all able to express what is within themselves. The key to being a Poet is to take what you have inside and put it on the outside. Everyone has an artist within them.

One way of awakening the Poet is to take up some form of art or craft and enjoy the process rather than the outcome. Instead of trying to accomplish something in particular, see if you can just enjoy the expression of your inner self. Art is a vehicle to awakening and expressing your inner senses; your sense of smell, texture, colour and sound.

Another way to awaken your inner senses is to put on your favourite dance track, close your eyes and really listen. Let your body sway to the back beat and enjoy yourself. Every time your mind wanders into the past or future, bring all of you attention into the music. Let yourself be fully in the moment. Forget what you look like and allow yourself to have fun.

Often if my wife and I have been working hard at home, we will grab our little girl, put her between us and dance around the room to some great music. The baby lights up and we all feel back in the present.

2. EMOTIONAL EXPRESSION

The other form of expression that is crucial to your well being is emotional expression. We all have ideas and feelings within us. One of the keys to becoming more of a Poet is to express them. Suppressing what you feel leads to unhappiness and losing the child within. Look at a baby – they don't suppress anything. They cry when they are unhappy and smile when they are happy. See how many times a day they smile?

I once saw a photograph of a whole row of babies that were smiling, accompanied by a whole row of old people that looked positively miserable. The caption read, "What happened?"

When you suppress one emotion you begin to suppress all of your emotions. If you put on a happy face for the world when you are sad, then eventually you will suppress your natural joy as well. All of your emotions are interconnected and it is important that your emotional muscles are exercised. Otherwise you begin to lose your get up and go.

Emotional expression is a subject that needs to be very clearly understood. Some people become almost totally ineffective because they allow minor things to emotionally swamp them.

Understanding the difference between "core emotion" and "churning" is the key to mastering the principle of emotional expression. I believe if you can learn to master this principle, your equanimity and happiness will soar.

CORE EMOTION VERSUS CHURNING

"Core emotion" is something that overwhelms you, like the death of a loved one. It is normal and human to express core emotion. Your tears are made of the same element as the Poet – water. If you dam your tears then you also block your Poet. And remember that just as you can have tears of sadness, you can also experience tears of joy.

If I ever meet someone who has recently had an extremely traumatic experience and they tell me that they are perfectly fine, I know they are either completely enlightened or they are avoiding their feelings. It is usually the latter.

"Churning" is a completely different scenario. Churning is when you create a strong emotion by constantly dwelling on something. For example, if you went to the local store and someone spoke to you a little harshly, you might dwell on it – "How dare that person speak to me like that?" If you turned it over and over in your mind, pretty soon you would have worked yourself up into being very upset.

I know people who have spent years in therapy just working on some minor issue. When I ask them what their intention is in seeking therapy, they tell me they have a problem and they just want to talk it over with someone. I reply, "Well you've certainly been successful then. What about an intention of clearing the issue and being happy?"

We are all human and if we encounter some frustration in our life it is normal to release it. However, you don't want to hang on to it. Going to the bathroom and eliminating is normal, but you don't need to examine it over and over again.

The reason you churn your emotions is because you are not clear on your intention or outcome. Sometimes the outcome is to seek attention or sympathy. If you have this particular outcome then it is very difficult to resolve your issues.

If your primary intention is to be happy, then you won't allow minor things to disturb you because this would run contrary to your primary intention.

I was giving a seminar one time when a man raised his hand to speak. He was visibly upset and trembling, on the verge of tears. We could all tell that he was feeling some core emotion that had been held down for some time. He was in a foreign army and had fought in three wars. He began to tell us that when he was twenty-three years old he had to guard the heavily wounded at night so the rats would not eat them. He was an officer and he would not give this duty to the eighteen year olds as he considered them too young for such an onerous task. Yet he was only twenty-three. As he related the story, tears were running down his cheeks. We were all touched deeply. As I looked around the room I could see a few people thinking that perhaps their life hadn't been so bad after all.

TRAITS THAT SELF-SABOTAGE

THE ONE-DIMENSIONAL POET

The undoing of the Poet comes about when someone refuses to awaken their other elements. Being a one-dimensional Poet and not achieving the Quintessence comes with a price.

The Poet who has an absence of the other elements cannot commit to any one person, philosophy or action. They often tend to be people who are on an emotional roller coaster. They are seeking the "perfect buzz." This often leads them into one relationship after another because they cannot deal with challenges and difficulties. If the relationship goes through a dry spell they start looking for the exit because "maybe someone out there is better".

You have probably met one of these one-dimensional Poets. Here they come, they're on cloud nine again. You wonder what is going to pop out of their mouth today. They look at you with stars in their eyes and say, "Wow, I'm so happy, I've finally found my soul mate."

"Yes I know," you reply. "You told me that last month."

They shake their head. "No, no, that was last month's relationship – this is *really* my soul mate."

Of course, what these Poets need is the Achiever to give them balance. Often, if they are confronted by their inability to commit, they might say something like, "You don't understand, I'm a free spirit, I need space to grow." or if they've *really* lost it, "I've got to be free so that I can spread inspiration and joy to everyone."

It is all about freedom for them. What the Poet doesn't understand is that freedom is achieved through commitment. Up until you are about twenty-eight years of age you are in a process of learning and discovery. Between eighteen and twenty-six you are in the advanced stages of adolescence. Adolescents by nature find commitment difficult. There are some people who know what they want from a very early age, but most people even at university level are still trying to find their own way.

Often, well-meaning parents force young people into committing to a career that may not actually be their passion. They may believe they are helping their child, but they are really assuaging their own fear of their children not settling into a steady income stream.

After the age of twenty-eight, your life lessons are learned through commitment and responsibility. If you master these two principles – commitment and responsibility – you become happy. You find that freedom on every level, from financial to spiritual, derives from these two principles. I have seen people who chase a spiritual high and end up getting caught in some cult. They are trying to achieve a spiritual experience from a leader or group. What they don't understand is that the "high" comes from within, and usually after many years of work. That is when it is real, when it is coming from within yourself. When it is coming from inside, no one can take it away, because it is yours.

The Poet seeks happiness. However, if you have ever met a forty year-old whose only developed element is the Poet, you have probably noticed they are not all that happy. They are still smiling on the outside, but they're starting to look a little battered and disillusioned. A lot of their dreams and ideals have not eventuated. The life they thought was effortlessly going to fall in their lap just hasn't happened.

There is another reason the one-dimensional Poet begins to look a little ragged around the edges. They often feel they cannot adequately protect themselves in any kind of confrontation. They sometimes feel that people take advantage of their generous nature. They avoid situations where they have to be assertive and as a result, miss many opportunities in life. The Achiever is assertive with people, and the Achiever is also assertive with themselves. An Achiever drives themselves on to their goal. It is this drive that the Poet lacks. If they are feeling passionate, there is no end to what they can do. However, if the passion is short lived, so is the project.

The strongest aspect of the one-dimensional Poet is the sense that they are insubstantial. You get the feeling that if you poked them in the chest your finger would go right through them. It is because they have not developed their Visionary Leader, an inner strength that comes from a core set of values and a mission in life. Those around them never fully know if these one-aspected Poets can be trusted or counted on in an emergency. Will they stick around or, like a butterfly, flit off somewhere else?

Many relationships with a one-dimensional Poet are wonderful in the beginning. Their partners claim they have never had so much attention or love, that is, until the Poet sees some other horizon and sets sail for a new island on a distant shore. They may still be physically in the relationship, but emotionally they have moved on.

The greatest difficulty for the Visionary Leader, the Achiever and the Sage is the ability to feel. The Poet in a sense gives life and animation to these three elements. However, for the one-dimensional Poet, feeling is not the problem. They feel everything. Many times they are simply overwhelmed by their emotions. Because they lack the other elements, everything just floods in. They take mildly sarcastic remarks deeply to heart. Watching a news bulletin of a current tragedy can not only reduce them to tears but throw them right off balance. They don't handle any kind of suffering well, including their own.

Imagine our one-dimensional Poet as a passenger in the back of a truck speeding over a very bumpy road. The bumpy road is their life during challenging times. They feel battered and bruised by the sharp movements of the truck. Because they cannot see outside, they have no idea where the truck is going or why the truck is on the road in the first place. All they know is that they want the truck to stop in a quiet meadow so that they can get out and sit and watch the flowers.

The Visionary Leader and Sage would allow the Poet to look outside the truck and see why they are being bumped around. They may suggest it's time to travel on a different road. Their Achiever would provide the tenacity they need to overcome the bumps on the road. However, when challenges arise in the life of the one-dimensional Poet, they just want them to stop or go away. They long for an idyllic world where everyone is happy all the time.

The problem with wanting challenges to go away is that the very reason you experience challenges is to teach you something. The more you resist learning lessons in life, the more aggressively those lessons pursue you. In running away, you actually run in a circle only to find your problem has compounded or changed form.

THE EXTRAORDINARY POET

One of my favourite poems that best describes the most sublime state of the Poet is by Christopher Morley. I have been reading this poem to groups now for many years. I always see a certain knowing look on people's faces, a remembering. We were once all poets. It is just a matter of rekindling our own inner poet. Here is the poem:

TO A CHILD

The greatest poem ever known
Is one all poets have outgrown;
The poetry, innate untold
Of being only four years old.

Still young enough to be a part
Of Nature's great impulsive heart
Born comrade of bird, beast and tree
And unselfconscious as the bee -

And yet with lovely reason skilled
Each day new paradise to build
Elate explorer of each sense
Without dismay, without pretence!

In your unstained transparent eyes
There is no conscience, no surprise:
Life's queer conundrums you accept,
Your strange Divinity still kept . . .

And Life, that sets all things in rhyme,
May make you poet, too in time -
But there were days, O tender elf,
When you were poetry itself!

Our four year old poet is "in the moment" – innocent, connected to life, love and passion, in total appreciation of themselves and their world.

THE SAGE

"How much wisdom have we lost with knowledge and how much knowledge have we lost with information."

T. S. ELIOT

HEIGHTENED PERCEPTION

I walked into a warmly lit room in the company headquarters. The space was long and rectangular. In the centre of the room was a very expensive timber and glass coffee table. The whole place had the scent of prestige, money and power. If this room had a name, it would have been known as "The special meeting room to impress people." If you worked for this company, this would be the room you would aspire to be in.

Around the coffee table were thick, luxurious lounge chairs, and on these were seated the chief executives of the company.

I had been asked into the company headquarters as a consultant. I hadn't been given any information on the company's financial position. All I had been told was that the company was looking to expand their horizons and develop their people. After I was formally introduced, the conversation moved to where the company saw itself heading and the bright prospects that the future could bring.

I knew from past experience that nothing really changes in life, business or relationships until you get to the truth. It seemed that this particular meeting was just going around in circles.

Finally I leaned forward in my chair and said, "Look, if it's okay with you, I'd like to cut straight to the chase." I looked directly at the Chief Accountant. "I bet if I looked at your books, I would find that if this company doesn't do something drastic in the next few years, you will be in liquidation."

An immense silence filled the room. The accountant looked at me in amazement and said, "Yes, that's true. How did you know that?"

"I felt it," I replied.

The accountant, puzzled, gently shook his head and said, "Well how do you do that?"

I looked at him and replied, "How do you not do that?"

What I meant was that this ability is a natural part of our makeup. We *naturally* have the ability to sense things but at some point many of us turn this sensibility off.

A few weeks later I was working with one of the Chief Executives in her office when she asked me, "Brendan, I notice that on many occasions you seem to have this uncanny ability to read situations and people like a book. You seem to know people's deepest thoughts. I feel that I lack that insight and it is limiting me in my life and career. How do you do it?"

"Okay," I replied, shifting in my chair to directly face her. "I want you to look at the desk and describe to me one object that is on the table."

After she described a pen to me, I asked, "So how do you know it's there?

"I can see it," she replied.

"So," I continued. "You trust what you see don't you? That's the first step in accessing your intuition or your knowing – you need to trust it as much as you trust all your other senses. If you heard a loud crash outside in the street you would have absolutely no doubt you heard it, so why doubt your intuition? When you awaken your Sage it is like turning on another one of your senses. Just like you trust what you see, hear and smell, you learn to trust what you feel. Imagine walking around constantly doubting what you see. Imagine how confusing that would be. Well, it's also confusing when you doubt what you feel."

She nodded in quiet, thoughtful agreement before I continued.

"You see, your intuition is like a friend. If you have a friend that constantly gives you advice that you never heed, what will your friend do?"

"They will either go away or keep quiet," she answered.

"Exactly," I replied. "If you listen to your intuition and follow it, then that friend actually becomes stronger and more powerful. It becomes a very powerful ally."

THE SAGE'S BLUEPRINT

Sages revel in a detached, dispassionate outlook. Perched on their mountain top they are able to view people without having to get involved in the emotional tides that engulf the rest of humanity. This is both their blessing and their curse as they can be largely without emotion in relationships. Like the Sage's element of air, you sometimes feel you can't get hold of them, as it is often hard to know what they are thinking and feeling.

Sages derive a tremendous fulfilment from observing people and contemplating the mysteries of life. This detached state gives them tremendous insight and clarity of thinking. However, without the emotion of the Poet, it limits their relationships. The Sage prefers an environment that is uncomplicated and ordered. They are by nature aloof and often reserved. To them, the gregarious Poet is just a little too over the top. A Sage will often find the wild emotional swings of the Poet and the headlong rush of the Achiever a bit disturbing. They often are quite happy in their own company and their quiet reveries.

THE POWER OF THE INVISIBLE

Air is the element you cannot see. All the other elements previously mentioned – fire, earth and water – can be touched and seen. Air, like intuition and wisdom, is invisible to the senses. However, just because it is invisible does not mean it isn't there. In our culture we put great emphasis on what can be seen, touched and felt and tend to distrust things that are not so tangible. "I need proof before I am going to trust something like intuition." is often the unspoken catch cry.

Air has the greatest mobility of all the elements. Like true wisdom and intuition it is free to move in any direction. Air will enter unseen into the smallest crack and sit in the shadows, like the watchful Sage. The Sage is quite content to let the Achiever and the Visionary Leader take centre stage. It prefers to remain invisible, watching and waiting in the background. You can often spot the Sage at a meeting or a party. They are the ones who appear dispassionate and reserved, but nothing escapes their attention. They wait until everyone has spoken before entering the fray with a stunning observation or comment showing perceptive lateral thinking.

Sages are masters of timing. They often take people with an undeveloped Sage by surprise because they have a tremendous capacity to wait before making their move. Sports people who abound in this element use it to pull a strategy out of the bag that is completely unexpected, thus giving them the winning edge. People used to say that Muhammad Ali "Floats like a butterfly, stings like a bee". The bee is the Achiever but the butterfly is grace, the Sage in action. Watching people at this level is like watching magic. Truly great sports people, such as six times world surfing champion Kelly Slater or golfer Tiger Woods, have the ability to do the seemingly impossible with an air of ease and grace.

A good example of this, and a real learning experience for me, was one of the first times I went rock climbing. We were halfway up a one thousand foot cliff face and on a vertical pitch of about one hundred feet. I could feel the sun on my back and the heat reflecting off the rocks, on to my hands and legs. My arms were beginning to tremble with the effort and sweat was dripping into my eyes. I was talking to myself, "Come on, push, you can do it, let's go." It was really taking all my focus and effort.

Even though I was securely roped and in little danger, I was clinging to the cracks in the rocks as if my life depended on it. As I finally clambered over the edge puffing and panting and congratulating myself for having made it, my friend said, "Check this out." As I got to my knees and looked up, there were two women climbers on the next pitch above. They were moving at a very easy but rapid, fluid pace. What was so stunning about them was that they weren't even breaking a sweat. They were just effortlessly snaking over the rocks. No straining, no grunting and heaving, just finding the perfect handhold at the perfect time. They were in the flow. Ease and grace. A small smile crept over my face and I shook my head in silent admiration.

INTUITIVE POWER

THE FIRST GREAT QUALITY OF THE SAGE IS *INTUITION*

Have you ever gone into a shop and tried on that shirt with the stripes and spots. As you're standing in front of the mirror with your face all screwed up wondering how quickly you can take off this ghastly covering, over walks the sales assistant.

"Oh, that looks wonderful on you."

You try to smile, but really you're cringing. It is obvious their Sage is either temporarily asleep or has gone on a long vacation. If their Sage was alert, they would have noticed everything about you and what you felt.

With a strong Sage, the sales assistant would just know what you were feeling. They would be more interested in steering you towards something you liked. They would also sense, after just a brief conversation, what budget you had. Rather than causing any embarrassment they would suggest certain options.

Truly great counsellors have a great blend of the Poet and the Sage. A friend of mine who is a renowned counsellor has the empathetic listening skills of the Poet. When she listens to you, you feel as if you are the only person in the world. However, she also combines this with a tremendous sense of wisdom. She rarely gives advice, but when she does it is always at the perfect time. She has an intuitive sense of when to speak and when to listen.

Intuition is the first great quality of the Sage. Your intuition is the voice of guidance. It has been referred to as a "gut feeling" or a "hunch". It warns you of impending danger or allows you to identify a situation that feels just right. It is a powerful ally and to be without it is a serious handicap in life. It is a valuable guide and dear friend. It is the primary quality and tool of the Sage. The Sage wielding the sceptre of intuition speaks in the ear of the Visionary Leader and the Achiever. It cautions them of impending roadblocks and alerts them to amazing opportunities. Millions of dollars have been made by legendary investors who have harnessed its capabilities. Romance has blossomed for those who have heeded an unexpected opportunity and whole new careers have flourished for those who have listened.

There are two voices within you that express themselves. The first is your inner dialogue and the second is your intuition. Your inner dialogue is the running commentary that manifests as inner chatter. Your intuition is a different voice altogether. For some people their intuition is a spoken voice. For most people though, it is a deep sense of feeling or knowing.

A good example of the two voices would be to imagine you had just finished a splendid, three course meal. As you sit there replete and completely satisfied, you notice there is one large slice of your favourite chocolate cake left on the table. Your internal dialogue might start saying "yes, yes, yes," while your intuition is saying, "If you eat that cake you're going to be ill."

I am often asked how I work out the difference between my inner dialogue and my intuition. Practices like meditation still the mind and the inner dialogue. As your mind becomes clearer and more focused by following these practices, you automatically know when your intuition is speaking. However, sometimes the messages may not be so clear. If that happens, proceed into the situation but keep listening to the messages.

Recently I was approached by a friend of mine to be part of a very large business venture. When I looked at the venture it seemed a fantastic opportunity, but as I began to proceed, all avenues to getting the project off the ground were blocked.

Opportunities that at first seemed promising finished in a dead-end. It felt as if there was no synchronicity at all. After several of these experiences I asked myself if these were merely hurdles we had to leap over, or if they were a genuine indication that this situation was not what I was meant to be doing. The more I *felt* into the situation, the more I became convinced that this venture was not for me. It felt that it was pulling me off my real track and my purpose.

I spent about two weeks of part-time work on the project before I finally arrived at this conclusion. I decided at that point to walk away, in spite of the fact that part of my inner dialogue was saying that I was walking away from a large sum of money. Months later the venture finally ground to a halt. If I hadn't walked away when I did I would have wasted months of time.

If you aren't sure whether it is your intuition or your inner dialogue that is speaking, you can listen to the quality of your inner voice. If it is an endless chatter in your mind, it is a good bet that you are hearing your inner dialogue rather than your intuition. Your intuition usually arises from a place of stillness within you.

BEYOND DOUBT

The biggest enemy of intuition is doubt. As Shakespeare said, "Our doubts are traitors." One kind of doubt is where you receive a strong intuition to go in a certain direction and then doubt its validity. I have lost count of the number of times people have told me how they acted against their intuition and as a consequence have had major learning experiences.

Another kind of doubt is where intuition itself is regarded as irrational and unscientific. When people refer to the god of science as being the paragon of rationality, I often remind them of Einstein's words, "I have not arrived at my understanding of the universe by means of the rational mind."

The rational mind is very important. We use it to do our taxes, figure out road maps and a host of other useful things. The rational mind provides us with clear thinking, which is essential in problem solving. This ability to think clearly is the most elementary level of the Sage. However, beyond this is a world that the rational mind cannot penetrate.

Some people hold the view that they can only believe in things that they can touch, hear and see. Yet science itself estimates that there is less than one billionth of our reality that can be recognised by our physical senses. A dog, for example, has a certain range of hearing that we do not posses. What we see is just a tiny fraction of what is actually there. In fact, the eye is a lens which perceives the world upside down. Our brain then turns the image the right way up. Our physical senses register only a narrow bandwidth of physical reality.

The rational mind is crucial to negotiate the problems of the world, however, it has its limitations. The intuitive mind *knows*. The rational mind *thinks* it knows. Intellectual understanding can only take you so far. You can study everything about the taste of chocolate but until you actually eat chocolate you will never truly know what it tastes like. When Carl Jung was asked if he believed in God he answered, "I don't believe in God. I know."

The Sage is often the most maligned and ridiculed of all the elements. In our culture there is a tremendous emphasis on phenomena being scientifically proven. The irony is that in the last hundred years, science itself has validated much of what intuitive people have known for a long time. These scientific discoveries have opened the door to seeing the world in a new light.

PERCEIVING ALTERNATIVE REALITIES

THE SECOND GREAT QUALITY OF THE SAGE IS THE *ABILITY* TO *PERCEIVE ALTERNATIVE REALITIES*

"Do I contradict myself? Very well then I contradict myself, I am large, I contain multitudes."

WALT WHITMAN

Perceiving Alternative Realities is the ability to break out of preconditioned thinking and see a different, more exciting world. The Sage can see alternative points of view in areas that most of us take for granted. Let's look at the principle of time. From one point of view, time is a highly measurable and stable commodity. Just get five accurate clocks, place them along side one another, and they will all happily record the same time hour after hour.

However, time is not as simple as it first appears. Time is a paradox. Einstein postulated that as an object increases its speed, it will experience a slowing of time. There was a very well known experiment where two atomic clocks were perfectly synchronised. One of these clocks was stationed in Switzerland, the other was flown around the world several times in a high speed jet. When the jet finished its journey, the clock in the plane read a slower time than its counterpart in Switzerland. The slower time had nothing to do with the vibration or force of the jet. It was purely because the clock within the jet was moving at a faster speed than the clock in Switzerland.

What this means in practical terms is that if you are travelling in a high speed jet looking at someone travelling on the earth on a motorcycle, you are ageing more slowly than the bike rider. However, the bike rider is ageing more slowly than a passing pedestrian who in turn is ageing more slowly than someone sitting on a park bench. All four are actually in different time zones or, to be more accurate, they are all in different "time space continuums". Scientists have realised that time and space are inextricably linked, so much so that they no longer use the word time on its own.

Of course, the difference in the time zones is minute as all four people are moving at relatively low speeds.

MYSTERIOUS MUONS

Let's see what happens if you actually move at higher speeds.

To get a completely different perspective on time we need to examine the mystery of muons. Muons are high speed particles that are invisible to the naked eye. They are created six kilometres above the earth's surface where the atmosphere of our planet begins. They travel at enormous speeds, in excess of 99% of the speed of light. Right now there are muons hitting you. The problem is that this is impossible. You see, muons only have a life span of two millionths of a second. If you do the maths on this, that is only enough time for the muon to travel half a kilometre. So how is it they can travel more than six kilometres? It is because the muon is moving so fast that time has slowed down, allowing the muon to reach you on earth.

If you took a 15 year journey in a space ship at 99% of the speed of light, you would experience first-hand the paradox of time. Let's say when you begin your journey you are 30 years of age. After travelling for 15 years you would return to Earth and be 45 years of age. For you, only 15 years would have elapsed. However, during those fifteen years, all the people on earth would have experienced time in a completely different way. When you finally arrive back on earth, every person you knew, including your children, would have died many years previously of old age.

BREAKING OUT OF YOUR REALITY BOX

"Reality is merely an illusion, albeit a very persistent one."

ALBERT EINSTEIN

If you think that time is a paradox, consider reality as we know it.

When Einstein said that reality is merely an illusion he was speaking in a very literal sense. Physicists have long known that the world we see is an illusion. How is this possible? The world that we see is made of matter which in turn is made of tiny particles known as atoms. Atoms are often thought to have a solid nucleus with solid particles rotating around the nucleus, much like our solar system where the planets rotate around the sun.

However, atoms are made up of particles that are not solid. They are energy. These little particles around the atomic nucleus – electrons – behave in strange and bizarre ways. First of all, the electrons don't have any particular position. The reason physicists can't tell you where they are is because there are random probabilities of the electrons' locations. In fact, one electron can occupy different locations at the same time.

Now, add to this puzzle a mind-blowing discovery. These particles only come into existence at the moment of observation. In a nutshell, all of matter comes into creation in the moment of observation. The closest physicists can come to explaining matter is with the maxim, "Matter has a tendency to exist."

"Quantum Physics ... has destroyed the concept of the world as "sitting out there." The universe will never afterwards be the same."

JOHN A. WHEELER

So, there you are admiring your brand new car. You can touch it, feel it and it definitely exists. Yet on another level the car and your body are just a series of particles. In fact, that is not correct either because the word "particles" implies something solid. You and your car are just energy.

If you really want to bake your noodle, lets take it one step further. Many physicists now believe that matter pulses in and out of existence. They believe that when it leaves existence it moves out of time. One minute the car is sitting there on the driveway, the next "second" it is somewhere else. So where is it really? If you look from the perspective of the Visionary Leader or the Achiever, you would get a single answer. It is either in the driveway or not. The correct answer, however, is both. On one level the car is there, on another level it isn't. Welcome to the world of the Sage. It is neither black or white. It is relative.

If all of this information is making your mind boggle, you are not on your own. Max Planck who won the Nobel Prize for physics said, "If anybody says he can think about quantum problems without getting giddy, that only shows he has not understood the first thing about them."

My suggestion to you is not to try to understand this with your rational mind. The rational mind can only take you so far. Planck himself tried for years to marry his discoveries with classical rational science before finally giving up. Beyond the mind there is a world that is so mysterious it cannot be grasped by reason.

The key to perceiving the world in all of its mystery is to let go of everything you know. The more you have what the Zen masters call "beginners mind," the more you can perceive the true wonder of the universe.

LIVING IN HARMONY WITH THE UNIVERSE

"The most beautiful and most profound emotion one can experience is the source of the mystical. It is the source of all true science."

ALBERT EINSTEIN

The Sage at the highest level perceives the world in a completely new way. In our culture the prevalent belief is that we are separate individuals. The average person believes that they begin and end at their skin. The highly developed Sage has the ability to see the world as an immense field of energy.

Indigenous cultures perceive the world as a vast interconnected field. I remember walking with a group of Aboriginal elders from the central desert of Australia. We walked a distance of three hundred meters from our campsite to a meeting place. The entire journey took nearly an hour to perform. As we walked every interesting plant and leaf was observed, and every step was savoured. The elders felt as if they were part of the entire landscape. It is a perspective that has allowed the Australian Aboriginal culture to live in harmony with the land for somewhere between 60,000 and 100,000 years.

To understand this difference in perspective, imagine walking with an Aboriginal elder on their traditional homeland. As you approach a group of trees you decide to sit under its leafy shade to rest from the hot noon sun. With your backs resting against the tree, you see a particularly beautiful eucalyptus twenty metres away. You turn to the elder and begin to describe this tree. You give a very accurate description of the dark brown bark, singed at the base from an old bush fire. From the trunk spread three distinct limbs covered in dusty green leaves.

The elder looks at you with eyes from another time and describes an entirely different scenario. She describes the tree in relationship to the tree you are sitting under and all the other trees in the nearby area. From the Aboriginal perspective, how can you describe one tree on its own when everything is related? They see nature as a cohesive, integrated landscape.

Our mechanical view of the world as a series of separate events has allowed us to make phenomenal technological progress. However, in the process, we have lost much of the mystery of life. Even when I listen to well-intentioned environmental groups, I sometimes see this separatist viewpoint. Some people believe they are trying to save something that is "out there". This is like a fish that is swimming in polluted water wanting to "save" the water. The fish and the water are inseparable. Without the water the fish would not survive.

Indigenous cultures don't see the world as "out there." They feel connected to the world. To them, a separatist viewpoint leads to loneliness. When you hold this separatist viewpoint it confines you to a narrow range of experience. The Sage is able to perceive themselves as part of this great interconnected field.

DIRECT ACCESS

I recall a time when I witnessed first-hand someone who had direct access to this interconnected field. My wife and I were studying with Pak Jero. Pak is a dukun; a healer, holy man and shaman rolled into one. He has calm twinkling eyes set in an oval face. He has the energy of a quiet, powerful dynamo and yet has the slowest, most deliberate walk I have ever seen. I often wonder if he even knows the meaning of "stress." We still visit him whenever we are in Bali.

Pak has embraced the Quintessence of unifying all five elements. He has a very strong sense of purpose, which he acts on to help the local villagers. He is a kind and compassionate Poet, knows who he really is, and has the deep and ancient wisdom of a highly evolved Sage. He is always quick to share a smile or a joke. Although he only speaks less than ten words of English, he has the ability to make a deep impact on people who speak halting Indonesian. He is so extremely "present" that outsiders who manage to find their way to his remote location often become agitated being around him. Like a still pond, he is a reflection of their own busy minds.

This particular time, we were sitting outside Pak's house on the raised wooden platform where he gave all his talks. Pak was wearing his traditional yellow sarong, an immaculate white shirt and a white headband. We were taking refuge from the intense tropical heat. We were talking about the area where we lived when Pak, in a very matter of fact tone, began to describe in detail the layout of our home. We had never told him, or any of the villagers, anything about our house, and he had never been outside of his own country, yet he was able to tell us from thousands of miles away what it looked like. Finally, at the end of his "tour" he described where my daughter's bedroom was and concluded saying, "Your daughter is busy with some project, she doesn't know I am in the room."

Pak was obviously not physically present in our house, however, some part of him was there with the ability to "see" inside.

The discoveries of physicists have confirmed what dukuns and shamans have understood for a long time, that energy seems to arise out of the very "nothingness" of space. It appears that there is some huge invisible energy field. From this field, particles of matter seem to come into existence only to eventually "decay" back into the field.

This vast energy field has been known to indigenous cultures and eastern mystics for thousands of years. Chief Seattle said in 1854, "All things are connected like the blood which unites one family. All things are connected . . . Man did not weave the web of life: he is merely a strand in it." The ancient Vaisesika philosopher Kanada of India talked of atoms, the relativity of space and time, and the dissolution of atomic particles, 2,800 years ago. Ancient cultures have known many things that we are only beginning to discover.

All of us have the ability to perceive our connection to a greater web of life. My wife's grandfather, who always regarded himself as a very conservative person, was so moved by a vivid dream he once had that he told the whole family. In the dream he was jogging in his familiar grey track suit when he collapsed on the sidewalk. As a group of people gathered around him, he had the sensation of looking down at his body and calling out to everyone, "Hey that's not me, I'm up here!" Three months later he was out jogging on the sidewalk, in his grey track suit, when he collapsed and died of a heart attack. As he lay on the footpath a crowd gathered over his body, just as he had seen in his dream, three months earlier.

The Sage who knows they are inextricably linked to this vast field of energy, is free to be part of that larger world. They experience a sense of freedom and expansion that is exalting. They know that the world is a wondrous place. From their standpoint they are not a single, lonely individual trying to find their place in the great scheme. Rather than being a solo violinist, they see themselves as part of a great orchestra. They belong to a universe that is in constant relationship. This sense of communion nourishes and inspires them.

AVOIDING DISASTER: FLEXIBLE THINKING

> *"I owe my success to having listened respectfully to the very best advice, and then going away and doing the exact opposite."*
>
> G.K. CHESTERTON

How does the Sage support us in a very real and practical sense in the world? Sages understand through their knowledge of alternate realities that to stay stuck in one point of view is to risk stagnation. Stagnation can lead to great personal distress as I witnessed first-hand when I was asked to lead a redevelopment program for government employees who were facing retrenchment.

I will never forget the first day of the course. As I walked to the front of the room and looked out at the faces of the workers, the message was the same from everyone. They were all frightened and bewildered. Many of them had been in their jobs for twenty or thirty years. None of them had ever expected this day would come. When they first became employees of the government they all assumed that it would be a job for life. In fact, for many of them, that was the very reason they joined in the first place. They wanted safety and security. They wanted to be in an environment that would never change.

Most of these people had bought an absolute. An absolute is when you hold a belief or position as certain and unchangeable. The following statements are good examples of absolutes:

> *"There is no reason for any individual to have a computer in the home."*
>
> KEN OLSEN, PRESIDENT OF DIGITAL CORPORATION IN 1977.

> *"Louis Pasteur's theory of germs is ridiculous fiction."*
>
> PIERRE PACHET, PROFESSOR OF PHYSIOLOGY AT TOULOUSE, 1890S.

When you *absolutely* know something to be correct you no longer allow new possibilities, and cease to be a lateral thinker.

The government workers were well meaning people who had clung to an idea that was no longer relevant. Living in that absolute had not prepared them for the rapid change of the late twentieth century and the new millennium. That absolute had brought about the very thing they were trying to avoid – change.

Wanting the world to stay the same is folly. One thing is certain: the world is constantly changing. That is the only constant in the world – change. The weather is sunny one minute and cloudy the next. This endless change doesn't only apply to small things. Great continents and mountains are shifting position and shape. The whole universe is in a constant state of change.

These days, things are moving too fast for us to hold on to absolutes. In 1900 the eighth largest company in America manufactured buggy whips. Where are they today? In this new millennium it will be imperative to embrace the Sage. Change is coming so quickly that we can no longer stick to old and outdated conditioning. For those who can embrace change and be fluid in their thinking it will be an amazing time.

The Sage gives you the ability to shift out of your preconditioned thinking and find new solutions. A lot of the time, what you perceive as the problem is not the actual problem. It is the way you *think* about the problem. Sometimes if you can expand your mind, the answer automatically comes to you.

I am sure you have had the experience of being stuck with a particular problem, with no possible solution in sight. You finally get so sick of it that you decide to do something else – go shopping, do the washing, anything to change the channel. As you're engaged in this new activity, out of the blue a solution that you would never have thought of comes to you.

Sometimes I am asked by people for a quick-fix solution. They want to know a specific technique to fix their relationship, or a quick remedy for their business or spiritual life. What they often want is to trade the absolute they are holding for a new absolute, but it is more important to first expand your mind. There may be several different answers to the same problem. The answer that comes from your inner knowing is usually the correct one. If you want to access this part of yourself it is important to transcend your absolutes.

In the world of the Sage there are no absolutes. Why? Because the Sage is more interested in wisdom than the accumulation of facts. When you strongly hold on to an absolute, your mind begins to contract. Try it. Begin thinking only in terms of absolutes for five minutes. Make some very strong mental assertions. People who are regarded as bigots are considered to be "narrow-minded." This is not just a figure of speech; the mind has the ability to contract and expand, and begins to contract when someone only thinks in absolutes. Their mind actually narrows or becomes less expansive.

A true Sage realises there are very few absolutes. Someone running may appear to be moving at a fast speed; however, compared to a cyclist they are slow. The cyclist compared to a car is even slower, and what about a jet? So, what is fast?

Let's look at the concept of large. I am what I would call an averaged-sized person. To an African pygmy I am a giant. Put me in a basketball team and I am a midget.

Lets look at the concept of up and down. Where in the universe is there an up and down sign? Someone standing on the north pole points toward their feet and says this is down. However for someone on the south pole the reverse is "true".

Fast, small, large, up and down are concepts. They only become real when compared with something else.

The Sage who can appreciate alternative viewpoints is open to lateral thinking and new possibilities.

AN EXERCISE IN LATERAL THINKING

One of the ways I used to train my children to have more lateral thinking ability is to give them certain exercises. Here is one of the puzzles I used to give them when they were little. Try it out.

An empty train pulls into a station and 20 people get on the train. It pulls into the next station and 5 people get off the train. At the next station, 10 people get on the train. The next station, 15 people get on the train. The next station, 5 people get off the train and at the last station, 10 people get on the train.

The question is, how many times did the train stop? The answer of course is six. However, the answer is largely irrelevant. What is more important is how people follow the problem. When I give most people the problem they start counting the numbers of people who get on the train. The reason they do this is that everything in their educational training has led them to follow this kind of procedure. A lot of our education is the accumulation of facts that we repeat back at exam time in the hope of getting good grades. Very little of our education is about thinking outside the square.

Einstein was a brilliant lateral thinker, but he couldn't read until he was seven and was described by his teacher as "mentally slow, unsociable and adrift in his foolish dreams". He was refused admittance to Zurich Polytechnic school. Thomas Edison was sent home from school with a note that said, ". . . this boy is too stupid to teach". The sculptor Rodin was the worst student in the school and regarded by his uncle of being incapable of educating. All of these people were well-endowed with the Sage. It was this element that allowed them to think outside the square and be an inspiration to the world.

BEING IN THE RIGHT PLACE AT THE RIGHT TIME

When you are in the right place at the right time, you are in touch with your own inner Sage. Whether they are a legendary investor who seems to have a "feel" for the market, or a sailor who senses the changing weather, the Sage is in tune with their environment.

I remember listening to a talk by the great mountaineer Doug Scott, who has climbed all the 8,000 metre peaks in the world. As he explained his adventures through his slide presentation, he pointed out all the mountaineers who had died over the years. By my count, it seemed nearly half of the people in those photographs had perished in the mountains. Finally, someone voiced the question of how he had survived into his fifties when so many others had not. In his quiet unassuming manner he leaned towards the crowd and said, "Because I listen. If it doesn't feel right, I do something else."

He explained that the final decision-maker is his intuition. If he gets a feeling to abort an attempt to the summit, then no matter how good the conditions look he will turn back. On the other hand, when climbing Everest, he got the feeling to make the final ascent at three in the morning. As it turned out, the weather held just long enough to reach the summit and return to the camp.

You don't have to be a mountaineer to use appropriate timing. *Appropriate timing takes the struggle out of life.* Sages have the ability to determine when to make their move. Like a great football quarterback, they stand holding the ball looking for the perfect opportunity to throw. Around them chaos reigns, with people running in all directions but the quarterback stands quietly centred, waiting for the appropriate time to act.

With their ability to perceive appropriate timing, the Sage makes life easy and graceful. It is this lesson of ease and grace that the Achiever needs to learn if they want to achieve holistic success.

A friend of mine who works in sales is a classic Achiever. He goes for everything like a bull at a gate, and often uses up twice as much energy than he would if he were to wait for the appropriate time. He rubs many people up the wrong way because he is not able to subjugate his ego and he barges in where Sages fear to tread. He means well but he starts becoming pushy and pretty soon customers start looking for the exit. Being a classic Achiever, all he sees is *outcome* and the sign above the customer's head that spells "target." He often wonders why people get upset with him and start becoming edgy. "Oh no, here comes that guy again." If he were to turn his Sage on, he would be able to determine what his customers really want.

When the Achiever combines with the Sage, it produces action and timing. It makes your passage in the world much easier.

SYNCHRONICITY

Have you ever had a day or a moment where you can't put a foot wrong? You seem to be in the right place at the right time. Everything just flows along as if the whole world is behind you. Actually, the world isn't behind you, you are with the world. As we know from our discoveries in quantum physics, the world is not made of inert material. The entire universe is one giant interrelated web. Each one of us is an integral part of that web.

Imagine yourself standing in a garden. If you look around the garden from a separatist, mechanical outlook, you see yourself and a series of individual plants, trees and flowers. However, let's look at the same scene from a quantum level.

As you look first at your own body, you see that it is comprised of a giant collection of energy particles that are in a constant state of recreation. From the mechanical point of view your body looks the same as it did a few minutes ago. However, from a quantum point of view the energy "particles" that made up your body are no longer there. They have been replaced with completely different particles. From this quantum view you recognise that you have a completely new body. As you look beyond the atomic particles you perceive a giant energy grid from which all of matter is being created. This energy grid is not just confined to your body, it extends out into the air in front of you and into everything in the garden. You no longer see yourself as separate, you see yourself as part of a vast flowing energy web that reaches into every fabric of the universe. You realise that you have always been connected to this grid.

Think of it as a large electricity grid. Rather than just relying on your own inner electric current, imagine how much power you can access when you plug into the whole circuit.

The key to achieving synchronicity is to first of all know that you are part of this grid. Once you know this then you will feel a link to everything around you. You will begin to act more on instinct as opposed to working everything out with your rational mind.

We have all had times when we have had a deep feeling to attend some event, only to meet someone there who influences our life in a very profound way. There is a tendency to explain this as a coincidence. What if there was some other force working behind the scenes?

Nine years ago my wife Annie and I received a phone call from a friend of ours. A well-known author was in town and our friend wanted to know if we could look after him and show him the sights. We spent the whole day with the author, John, and had a great time. At the end of the day he said to me that if I ever decided to write a book, I should phone him. We never saw John again and lost all contact with him.

About a month ago, my wife and I were talking about John saying that we should get hold of him as we wanted some advice on this book. We couldn't recall what state he lived in, nor did we currently know anyone who knew him. The next morning, when Annie walked into the office she saw a box of old papers and business cards that our baby daughter had turned over. There at the top of the heap was John's card. It had been buried in the bottom of the box. We hadn't seen that card for nine years and had forgotten we had ever received it. We contacted John that day who was very pleased to hear from us. He remembered our conversation and said he would be delighted to help.

These "coincidences" in our life are a natural occurrence. When you embrace the Sage they begin to happen to you more and more frequently. They are an indication that you are in the flow of life.

The real beauty of synchronicity is that life takes on a deeper meaning. You experience a sense of purpose and a belonging to a greater force. You discover that life is not something to be figured out and filed, but a mystery to be experienced.

ACTIVATING YOUR INNER WISDOM

The vast grid of energy that creates matter is in itself alive. It has, for want of a better word, an intelligence or knowing. When you align yourself with this "knowing," you begin to automatically understand things about people and places. You begin to feel directed to move along certain pathways. You activate your inner wisdom.

The key to being a Sage is to move away from making decisions based on a logical, fixed state of mind. I remember learning this lesson the hard way.

Many years ago I invested some money in a managed fund. I was so excited about the promised returns that I ignored some inner alarm bells. The track record of the company was impressive and I overrode my inner feelings. Several months later the company went into liquidation and most of my money disappeared. In hindsight, I realised that what I had allowed my ego to override my intuition. In essence it was like saying to the universal grid, "I don't need to listen. I can go it alone. I don't need you!"

If you want to be a Sage then you need to allow yourself to be directed by your intuition. Your intuition will give you the gift of synchronicity to let you know you are on the right track. When you are on the correct track you will run into the right people at the right time. You will pick up a book and turn to the exact page you are meant to read.

If you are not on the right track, the exact opposite condition can happen. All of a sudden everything can go horribly haywire. Everywhere you turn you meet obstacles and drama. This does not mean that every time you have a negative experience you are off track, but it can be an indication to you that you need to reassess the situation. You have to take a look at the whole picture in context.

In general, I find people who have committed to a path of self-improvement will experience synchronicity when they are on track and its opposite state when they are off track. The Divine Force is benevolent in nature. It is not out to punish you for wrong doing or being misguided. However, in that benevolence "it" knows that when you are on track you are more fulfiled and happy. If you stray too far off the path, you may receive signs to correct your life. The break up of my first marriage was a good example, and something that inspired me to look deep within myself. Sometimes what you perceive as a negative experience is actually a wake-up call, to get you back on track.

A WAKE-UP CALL

One of the greatest examples of not listening to your intuition can be seen in the life history of the humanitarian Buckminster Fuller. "Bucky", as he was affectionately known, was one of the most prolific inventors of the 20th century. He was someone who, through his work, embraced the Quintessence. However it hadn't always been that way.

When Bucky was a young man his family pooled their resources and raised enough money to send him to Harvard. Within a short period of time Bucky became very bored and went to New York in search of a good time. He found a musical on Broadway, and at the end of the show took the entire female cast of dancers out to the most expensive restaurant in the city. In that one night he blew his entire savings. Harvard found out about this exploit and expelled him.

His family decided that Bucky needed to learn the error of his ways, so they sent him to a Canadian woollen mill that an uncle had an interest in. Because he was a prolific inventor, Bucky was able to fix the machines in the mill in record time, so much so, that the local newspaper printed a story on their new hero. His family sent the clipping to Harvard, explaining that Bucky had reformed. Harvard took him back but it wasn't long before Bucky was up to his old tricks and he was subsequently expelled once more.

For years Bucky roamed around seemingly lost and out of place. Nothing seemed to work out for him. By now he was married and had a four year old daughter, Alexandria, who had been very sick from birth. One day he received a call from his old Harvard buddies who wanted him to come and see the Harvard-Yale football game. When he asked his wife if he could go, she looked at him and asked him if he was going to behave. She knew his reputation for enjoying a good time. She said that if it was okay with Alexandria, it was okay with her. Going upstairs, he peered over Alexandria's bed and asked her the question. She looked up at her father and said, "That's fine with me Daddy, but can you bring me back a flag?" Bucky said he would bring back her present, and he took off to the game.

To this day, no one knows if he made it. It was party time once again for Bucky. Three days later he returned home to a distressed wife. She looked at him and said, " Where have you been? Alexandria has been very sick."

He tore upstairs and there was Alexandria burning up with a fever. He reached down and picked her up in his arms.

She opened her eyes and looked at him. In a feeble voice she said,

"Daddy, you're back. Did you bring me my present?"

A chill settled over Bucky as he hesitated. "No, I forgot."

A look of disappointment crossed her face. She closed her eyes, went into a coma and eventually died.

Bucky said much later that some people get the message with a feather and others with a Mack truck. That was Bucky's Mack truck and the turning point in his life. He eventually entered a two year period of almost total silence in the quest for finding inner truth. In reassessing his life he was able to get back on track, and eventually inspire audiences around the world with his forward ideas and benevolent concern.

THE SAGE'S TOOLKIT

DEVELOPING YOUR INTUITION AND INNER KNOWING

A lot of the time you may not be receiving dramatic messages about whether your life is on track or not. Many people receive just one long message. The message shows up in their lack of fulfilment in the major areas of their life.

I know a woman who for years has been complaining that their relationship, career and spiritual life is unfulfilling. It isn't as if anything is going particularly badly in her life; however, nothing is really great. It is obvious to the friends of this person that her commitment to their evolution, perfectly matches the results they are getting in the world. Their Sage is going, "Hey, maybe you need to change course." However, she's just not listening.

If you want to check to see if you are listening to your inner guidance, run through the Life Check List and have a look at the following major areas of you life:

THE LIFE CHECK LIST

Spiritual life
Relationship
Family life
Career, Finances
Recreation, Hobbies, Personal life
Contribution to humanity.

Ask yourself, "Do I feel fulfiled in all of these areas?" One way of getting a totally honest answer to this question is to rank your feelings of fulfilment in each area on a scale from one to ten, ten being the highest score possible and one being the lowest. Say, for example, you put a score of three for your personal life. Ask yourself, "Have I been working too hard and ignoring an inner feeling to have some fun?" If you put a low score on your relationship, perhaps you have been ignoring an inner urge to spend some quality time with your partner. You will usually find a direct correlation between ignoring an inner guidance and the feeling of being fulfiled.

Sam was a participant in one of my seminars. He had short black hair, intense eyes and a direct, honest demeanour. The only area of his life where he felt fulfiled was his career. Needless to say, his only awakened element was fire – the Achiever. As he learned to embrace his Sage, he was able to listen more to his inner needs and feel fulfiled in other areas of his life. Prior to this, his relationship with his family was practically non existent. He set out to rectify the situation and now has a great relationship with both of his sons.

As he looked at the Life Check List above, he realised that the piece that was missing most was his spiritual life. He had come from a very poor family and had accumulated a level of material wealth that most people dream of. He was rightfully proud of what he had achieved but felt empty. He turned the incredible focus of his Achiever in a spiritual direction. He began to meditate and attend some of my advanced seminars that deal with the issue of spirituality. Today, Sam radiates an air of contentment. His employees, who were once frightened of him, now work out of a genuine sense of loyalty.

His business is more successful than it has ever been.

Think of your Sage as a regulator or chief of operations. This chief sends out messages to all your other elements, informing them what to do. When you apply your intuition to the other elements, you tap into a very powerful force. You no longer act out of your own individual strength. You act as part of the great web and in essence have the assistance of that vast energy grid. You feel as if you are being directed by some larger force, being led rather than pushing and struggling to achieve your goals.

It is like a skier who is laboriously climbing a mountain, struggling with all their might to reach the top. As they glance overhead, through the sweat dripping off their brow, they see another skier riding a chairlift, leaning back enjoying the view.

Mother Teresa put it very beautifully when she called herself, "a pencil in God's hands".

FOUR STEPS TO DETERMINING IF YOU'RE ON TRACK

If you are now clear on what is important in the major areas of your life, how do you gain clarity in individual situations? For example, let's say that "career" ranked very high in your Life Check List. You have just started a new venture or project but are not sure if you are travelling down the right road.

Try the following steps:

STEP 1

Remember when we discussed Grand Purpose in the Visionary Leader? The first step is to ask yourself if the project or situation is an aid to your Grand Purpose. Is this project something that would enhance your growth? Is the situation in line with your vision? Is it an appropriate vehicle to aid your evolution?

I remember talking with someone who had once had an extra-marital affair. The affair did an immense amount of damage to his marriage. As he looked back on his actions, he was able to see that the affair was not an aid to his evolution. It had been an impulse of his mind and emotions rather than his intuition.

STEP 2

See if you have genuine passion or enthusiasm for the project. The word enthusiasm is derived from 'Theos' which means God. When you follow genuine passion or enthusiasm it may be an indication that you are following in the plan of God or the Divine Force. I know with my work, it rarely feels like work. It is something that I love to do.

STEP 3

See if there is some synchronicity involved in the project or situation. When a situation is on track, magical coincidences are a natural occurrence. I know even in writing this book that a certain piece of information would appear at exactly the moment I needed it. Once I was searching for a quotation that would describe what I was working on. Having no luck I decided to take a break. I walked out of my office and my wife, who was sitting in front of her computer, said, "I found this on the internet, would this be of value for your book?" It was the exact quote I was looking for. When this kind of synchronicity happens it let's me know that I am on the right track.

If you are involved in something where there is no synchronicity, it may be that you have hit an obstacle. This is when you need the Achiever to help you keep going. Often, if you keep persevering, synchronicity will begin to occur. However, if everything continues to be a struggle then you might need to examine your motives for being involved in the situation. This is a very fine line. Sometimes it may be that you are being tested. If you just keep going, success might be over the next hill.

STEP 4

Keep *feeling* into what you are doing. Does it feel good? Keep trusting that inner feeling and allow it to become a close friend. Remember that just because your intuition is not tangible, it doesn't mean it doesn't exist. You cannot see radio waves, yet that doesn't mean they don't exist. All you need is to tune into the correct frequency to pick up your inner feelings.

BUILDING YOUR INTUITIVE MUSCLES

A great way to develop your intuition is to use your Achiever to act on your intuitive messages. The faster you act, the stronger your intuition becomes. It is like a great sports person who trains their reflexes. As their reflexes become faster and faster they trust their instincts more and more. A friend of mine who is a high ranking martial artist practices the same elementary drills over and over so he can go beyond the stage of thinking, to instinctive action.

Do you remember how awkward driving was when you were in the car for the first time? You had to think about every single movement. Now you find shifting gears and negotiating traffic is an automatic response. The difference with racing drivers is that they train their instincts to act as soon as possible. The faster they can act, the better racing drivers they become. Intuition is the same. The faster you act the stronger your intuition becomes. In essence you are sending a very clear message to your intuition that says, "I trust you." Like any relationship, the more trust there is the stronger it becomes. This is one way of training your intuitive muscles. Another very powerful way is what I call "seeing things as they are".

SEEING THINGS AS THEY ARE

If you want to have a high level of mastery of your intuition, you must be willing to see a situation as it really is, rather than what you would like it to be. The open-hearted Poet trusts everyone. *Highly intuitive Sages don't trust people, rather they trust what they feel about people.* In this way, they avoid delusion.

Delusion occurs when you don't see a situation or person as they really are, and works in two different ways. One way operates through naivety, for example when someone who is naive trusts the wrong person. The other way can be seen in someone who has, for example, had a very bad relationship experience and believes that all members of the opposite sex are not to be trusted. They come to a conclusion based on their past experiences.

However, delusion can be much more intrinsic than these examples. Harvard University undertook a study in which they raised two groups of kittens. The first group was raised in an environment solely containing vertical stripes. The second group was raised in an environment where everything contained horizontal stripes. When the kittens became cats, they were placed in a normal environment.

The group that had been raised in a vertically striped world were unable to see anything that was horizontal. If, for example, there was a low lying coffee table, they would bump into the table top. The group that were raised in a horizontal world, on the other hand, were unable to see anything vertical and would bump into the table legs.

The cats had been conditioned to perceive the world in a certain way. All of us have been conditioned to see the world from our own distinct viewpoints. The art of having a high level of intuition is to go beyond your conditioning. It entails perceiving a person or situation without being influenced by your conditioned mind. It means using your intuition to directly see a particular scenario.

With a high level of intuition you, are able to do this with everyone in your world. Even the people that are close to you. If you hold one thing in delusion or fantasy, it affects your entire sense of reality. It is like wanting to be extremely fit and running ten miles every morning, then smoking a packet of cigarettes every night. Those cigarettes are going to affect your fitness. Even if you increase your fitness program, unless you ditch the cigarettes, you will never really achieve peak fitness. It's the same with your intuition. If you hold one thing in delusion, it will cloud your intuition in other areas.

To get out of delusional thinking, you need to see people and situations as they really are, rather than what you would like them to be. It takes a lot of courage to do this. Human beings often hold delusional thinking as a way of protecting themselves. I remember talking to someone who refused to believe that their partner would let them down. Even though deep down they intuitively knew the truth, it was too painful for them to face. Later, when the relationship broke up they had to face the truth, which was that their partner had never been committed to the relationship.

Delusional thinking can also inhibit you from feeling a strong sense of self. A person I know who is a classic Poet often felt taken for granted in her relationships with people. She felt that people treated her as doormat because she allowed them to walk all over her. She trusted people that any discerning person would never trust. She is now learning how to establish healthy boundaries and stand up for herself, which is giving her a sense of strength and confidence. Essentially, she is awakening her Sage and her Achiever. When the Sage and the Achiever form an alliance it gives you a very powerful form of protection. The Sage evaluates people's true intentions and the Achiever backs up those intentions by creating firm boundaries.

A friend of mine who is very successful in business has the ability to see everything as it really is. If he is looking at a new proposal, he never allows himself to be swayed by hype or popular opinion. It is one of the traits that has made him successful.

One area where delusion is at its greatest, concerns some of the more questionable cults. People who are in hope, seeking answers to life's difficult questions, project an image of their own making onto the group leader. They see the group leader as perfect and someone who will never let them down, which is a fantasy. We are all human and projecting something onto someone that isn't real only does yourself and the other person a disservice.

The real key to having powerful intuition is to be able to see the truth of who someone really is, not who you would like them to be. Of course, you also need your Visionary Leader to see the person's potential, however the Sage is interested in seeing things as they really are. When you develop this ability to a high degree, it allows you to attract people who can aid your plans and help fulfil your goals.

TRAITS THAT SELF-SABOTAGE

THE ONE-DIMENSIONAL SAGE

Have you ever looked from above at a trail of ants? As you watch the ants it is like peering into another world. This is often how the Sage sees the world of human relationships.

People whose only aspect is the Sage are very aloof. They tend to stand back and observe the world from a distant view-top. They see all the comings and goings of humanity, but they never feel emotionally involved. To them it is a vast movie, fascinating, interesting and intriguing. If the Sage lacks the Poet then the problem is further acerbated. They simply find it difficult to feel, and become detached from those around them. This, of course, plays havoc with their relationships. In the beginning they are admired for their incredible insight into problems. Grateful partners delight at their ability to get right to the heart of the matter. However, as time goes on, their calm dispassion becomes a thorn under the skin.

One of the keys to success in relationships is the sharing of emotions and feelings. The one-dimensional Sage finds this a daunting tasks. Because of their tremendous insight, they see everyone's foibles. However, without the Poet's compassion, they fail to realise that we are all on an evolutionary journey.

The one-dimensional Sage who does not have the benefit of the Achiever never really rises to their potential. They often have a great depth to them, and they know exactly what they should do, but the problem is actually doing it. Without the drive of the Achiever there is no incentive to go out and make something happen. They might see an opportunity right in front of them, but without the Achiever they find it hard to dive through that window.

THE EXTRAORDINARY SAGE

COMMUNING WITH CLOUDS

We were just outside of Taos, New Mexico, on a very cold mid winters day. It was alternating between rain, sleet and the occasional flurry of snow. We had taken a select group to meet some of our Native American friends. Most people would call them medicine men/women or shamans, yet I have never heard any authentic medicine person ever refer to themselves by this name. Humility seems to be their hallmark. Most of them would say something like, "I'm just here to pray for the people, to give a little help".

Our group were driven inside the house by the freezing conditions. We had all come to participate in a Native American sweatlodge which was to be run by a medicine man I will call Martin, who lived on a reservation several hours away. (A sweatlodge is a ceremony which physically feels a bit like a sauna, but has a very powerful and sacred atmosphere.)

Martin looks like any other Native American. His long black hair falls down his back. If you saw him in a crowd you probably wouldn't even notice him – medium height, round face with inquisitive, owl-like eyes. He tends to be a listener rather than a talker and has a very quiet unassuming manner. When it is time to do the ceremony, however, he is always completely focused and in command.

It was about an hour before we had to light the fire to heat up the large rocks that were to be brought into the confines of the lodge itself. As I looked around the group I could see some of the members were wondering how we could light a fire in these cold, wet, sleeting conditions.

When Martin came into the house that day, many people didn't even see him. He wandered over to a small cluster of people standing just outside the kitchen.

In this group was a friend of ours who had joined the tour by the name of Brian. We used to joke to Brian that he was so conservative that banks would reject his employment application because he was too straight. Brian had come on the trip to broaden his horizons. He was a bit sceptical about all this stuff but he was genuinely giving it his best shot.

Brian struck up a conversation with Martin and they were talking amicably enough when Martin looked at Brian and said, "You'll have to excuse me, I need to go and handle the weather".

Brian just looked like someone had said, "We are eating roasted bats for dinner." A cross between disbelief and "What did he just say?"

Martin went outside and began to ceremoniously chant quietly to himself and the elements.

About 25 minutes later a ragged hole appeared in the clouds above us. For several miles in every direction, it ceased to rain or snow. Everywhere outside that rough circle the weather continued to come down. It stayed that way while we lit the fire and throughout the several hours of the ceremony. About half an hour after we finished, we were covered in flurries of snow. It had all happened so inconspicuously that some of the group hadn't even noticed.

What was the reason for this "miracle?" Because this group had come such a long way and with genuine good intention in their hearts, Martin just "wanted to help the people".

Brian still talks about it to this day.

Martin is someone with the element of the Sage at a very rarefied level. He knows that he is part and parcel of the great dance of life. Rather than seeing himself as separate to all of nature, he actually experiences nature as part of himself. He experientially knows he is part of the great web of life. This is not a theory, it is a way of being.

The elements of nature are like friends to him.

One medicine man I know who is in his fifties, started his training when he was six years old. It is not something you just study out of a book, it is an entire way of being. Someone who can work with nature will humbly request its co-operation; they never demand it. It is all about respect. If you had developed a strong group of influential friends, you might request favours from them. If you arrogantly demanded things from them they would probably go elsewhere.

The consummate Sage is in the flow of all things. They do not barge through brick walls, they move in harmony with everything around them. Elegance and grace.

Some people find the story of Martin and the weather absolutely amazing. While I am amazed, I have seen things like this many times, in several countries. Why? Because I expect to see them.

The key to having more experiences like this is to be open to them. Quite a few people close themselves off from other experiences because it is too confronting. They want to feel safe in a world that is structured and ordered. It is a way of staying in control. However, the world isn't fixed. It is constantly changing. When you let go of control you realise there is nothing to fear.

It is like sitting in a large room, facing a corner. As you stare at the walls, you believe that all that exists in your universe is this one corner. Along comes the Sage who takes you by the hand and says, "Yes, that is a very interesting corner, but if you just change your angle of vision you will see an entire room." You turn your head and all of a sudden you see an array of wonders you had never noticed before.

SPIRIT

"We are not human beings having a spiritual experience. We are spiritual beings having a human experience."

TEILHARD DE CHARDIN

THE POWERFUL PRESENCE

We had been awake all night. It was the birth of my first daughter, Elesha, and the small group who were assembled in the birthing room were working together as a cohesive unit, quietly and efficiently taking care of all the necessary details.

Leading up to this birth none of us realised that on this particular day we were to experience a lesson that would alter our perception of the way we viewed people and the world around us.

As the rest of the city lay asleep, we were immersed in another world. The intensity of the moment had banished all thoughts of the past and the future. We were all firmly rooted in the present. It seemed nothing else existed outside that small dimly lit room. Conversations were brief and muted. All of us were witnessing one of life's greatest miracles — birth. The contractions became more frequent and powerful. I looked around the room and could see that everyone's concentration had risen to another level, adding to the mounting pressure. The intensity was so thick you could have cut it with a knife.

Finally the moment arrived. The baby slid out uttering a little moaning cry "oh oh oh". It sounded for all the world like, "I'm here, thank God that's over, I'm here." There was no distress in the sound.

Rather it was as if the baby was relieved it was all over. After the baby was helped up on to her mother's stomach we waited for a while to let her settle.

20 minutes later I took Elesha in my hands. I could feel the incredibly soft, silky skin and the almost weightless feel of her body. Very slowly I eased her into a tub of water that was slightly warmer than the amniotic fluid in the womb. Seven adults were on one side of the portable bath while I was on the other. It was then that something completely unexpected occurred.

As Elesha lay in the water, she opened her eyes completely. Being twenty minutes old, she couldn't move her head, but her eyes moved to each person in the group. She looked at each person for up to several minutes at a time. This was not the fuzzy-eyed, defocused look of a new-born, but the intense and intent gaze of a completely aware being. After looking deeply into the eyes of one person she would move to the next person and gaze profoundly into their eyes. Throughout this time her eyes never wandered vacantly into space. They remained firmly focussed on each individual. Looking into the baby's eyes was like staring into the depths of a naked soul — a vast powerful presence.

It was completely apparent to everyone that Elesha was the oldest and wisest being in the room. It was as if we were in the presence of someone who was centuries old.

It took a few days for this to change. After two days, Elesha became a baby, manifesting all the innocence of every new-born.

In India they say that at the moment of birth, Maya throws her net over you and you begin to forget who you really are. Maya is the net or web of illusion. What you forget is that you are a spiritual being. You begin to slowly turn your attention to the external events in the world and identify with them. You see yourself as your body, emotions, feelings and achievements. The more you identify with all these things, the more your true essence becomes clouded and obscured. You travel through life feeling that something is missing, that no matter how much you achieve, something eludes you. Many people never realise that what eludes them is closer than their own breath, nearer than their own skin. It is their own Spirit.

WHAT IS REAL?

Just as we constantly change our clothes, our bodies are also constantly changing. The body you inhabit right now is biologically entirely different to the one you inhabited three years ago. Every cell and molecule is completely different.

It is not only your body that is in a constant state of change. Your thoughts and beliefs are different from those you had when you were a child. At seven, you viewed the world in a different manner than you do now. Have you noticed that what you were so certain of years ago, may now seem absurd? You are probably familiar with the humorous remark I have often heard at my seminars: "When I was eighteen I always considered my parents quite wrong and stupid. By the time I reached twenty-eight I was amazed at how much intelligence they had gained in ten years."

If our bodies, thoughts, beliefs, opinions and emotions are constantly changing, then we have to ask the question "What is real?" Anything that is in a constant state of change cannot be classed as real. From reading about the discoveries made by quantum physicists in the chapter on the Sage, you know just how little is real.

The only thing that is real and unchanging is your essence, your being, your Spirit.

CONTACTING YOUR SPIRIT

The experience of contacting your Spirit or your soul is the feeling of a still mind and a vast sense of beingness. Alfred Lord Tennyson, the Poet Laureate of England, gave a description of his own experience of contacting his Spirit:

> *"A kind of waking trance have I frequently had from boyhood onwards, when I have been all alone. This has generally come upon me through repeating my own name two or three times to myself silently till all at once, as it were, out of the intensity of consciousness of individuality, the individuality itself seemed to dissolve and fade away into boundless being, and this is not a confused state, but the clearest of the clearest, the surest of the surest, the wisest of the wisest, utterly beyond words, where death was a laughable impossibility, the loss of personality (if so it were), seemingly but the only true life. I am ashamed of my feeble description. Have I not said the state is utterly beyond words?"*

The state of residing within your Spirit is to experience total clarity and awareness. Your personality takes a back seat and is replaced by the feeling of beingness. Fear vanishes as you realise that who you really are is a deathless infinite being. This state is known by many names. In Zen, they use the word "Sartori" to describe the state when you get a glimpse of your true essence. The Tibetans call it "the view" because you perceive the world in a completely new way and with an added heightened perception.

> *"From the unreal lead us to the Real"*
>
> THE UPANISHADS

In one of my seminars we were working on this one element — getting to the core of who we are. The participants were undertaking an experiential process that took each person to themselves. Slowly the room became quieter and quieter. A deep calm began to emanate from everyone as people's thoughts ground to a halt. For over half an hour no one spoke. It was as if words were completely unnecessary. Later when we discussed it, each person voiced similar thoughts. "It was as if I was right there inside myself, all along, just waiting to find myself."

Someone else said, "I realised at the point of finding myself, that I was really identical to everyone. It was just me looking at me." There were many nods of acknowledgement from those who had felt the same thing.

WHAT IS SPIRITUALITY?

If you take a hologram of a swan and smash it into hundreds of pieces, you will see the whole swan in each individual piece, not just a part of the swan. Every one of those pieces will contain the whole bird. If you think of the Divine Force or God as a giant hologram, each one of us is a particle of that Divinity. True spirituality is recognising your own Spirit so that you can then realise you are part of a greater force. True spirituality is when you connect with your true nature, your Spirit, which enables you to connect with the Divine Force.

"That which is born of Spirit is spirit"

JOHN 3:6

The word religion originally comes from the Latin *religio* which means bond. The word yoga derives its origin from the Hindu Sanscrit "union." They both have the same meaning: to bond or create a union of your true self, your Spirit, to the Divine Force.

Just as you are part of the flow of the river of life, you first need to realise that you are a drop of water before you can realise you are the river. Imagine a drop that defined itself as a cluster of hydrogen and oxygen atoms. It is akin to a human defining themselves through their thoughts, personality and emotions. You are so much more than that. You are vast and infinite. When the drop understands its true nature, it is then able to comprehend the river.

Spirituality takes your beyond the mind. It transcends all philosophies and belief systems. It is a state rather than a creed.

> *"The currents of the Universal Being circulate through me,*
> *I am part and parcel of God"*
>
> EMERSON

To touch your Spirit you have to go beyond your intellect, beyond a prescribed process and beyond a spiritual practice. The process might take you to your Spirit, but the process itself should not be confused with the destination. In the same way, medicine may restore your natural health, but you would not say that a state of health *is* medicine. A spiritual path is the path that takes you to the destination. It is very seductive to mistake the path for the end goal. Wars have been fought because opposing sides became fixated on their path or religion, rather than the goal.

What you are really trying to find through spiritual practice is the place of origin. You are trying to find your real essence. It is not some new place you are developing. It has always been there, like a secret garden of renewal, waiting to be discovered.

A good spiritual practice will take you beyond the thoughts of the mind towards your real self. The best practices are the ones that produce results, that bring you closer to your true nature.

PERSONALITY DEFINED

As you move into the world, you slowly connect yourself with people and the things around you. You develop a personality and begin to forget who you really are — a being or spirit, a particle of the Divine Force. Most people, however, view themselves through their personality.

Your personality is an important part of your make-up. It is essential on this physical plane to have one, as it dictates how you relate to people. However, your personality is not who you *are*. For example, you may wear a smart suit to an important meeting; however, you wouldn't walk around thinking that you are a smart suit. If you did think you were your clothes, you'd probably be considered narcissistic or insane. Yet this is the situation you commonly find. People often grasp at ephemeral notions, believing they are their bodies and personalities. This is probably the most extreme form of narcissism.

Your personality is made up of a series of identities. An identity is a role you assume in order to function in the world. Some of these identities may be ways you describe yourself, such as, strong, courageous, weak, determined, cunning, straightforward, etc. You may also define your identity through your professional role in the world, such as a dancer, businessperson, doctor, singer or baker; or perhaps your family role of mother, father or grandparent.

In essence, an identity is the way you define yourself to others. The more strongly you believe in that definition, the more that identity becomes fixed into place.

Your identity will determine your behaviour. Let's say that someone believes they are a "tough guy." Imagine that they have believed this so strongly that it has become a fixed identity. This identity will then dictate certain behaviours. Perhaps these behaviours are unfriendliness, hostility or aggression.

Recently in a training seminar, we were discussing identities and behaviours when Joan, a woman in her sixties, spoke about one of her very strong identities. Joan said that all her life she had felt compelled to be loving and caring even when she didn't want to be. She felt that her entire family saw her as someone that was selfless, and that they often took her for granted. When I asked her why she stayed with this identity she replied that it was her way of feeling good about herself. She also said that she enjoyed being perceived as selfless, loving and caring.

As we explored the issue, she realised that this identity was so strong that it was trapping her into certain behaviours that were not in her best interests. She realised that she wasn't able to be flexible in her behaviour and say no to people.

Many people hold steadfastly to an identity because it is the source of their self-esteem. Like Joan, who 'scored points' from those around her for having a certain behaviour, people hold certain identities to give themselves a sense of self worth.

Let's look at this concept of self worth or self-esteem.

GAINING TRUE SELF-ESTEEM

There has been much written on self esteem but what is it?

Many people find the following exercise extremely powerful in discovering the true nature of self-esteem. Mentally list, or write in the space below, what you consider are the sources of your self-esteem.

I get my self-esteem from:

____

____

____

____

You may have written achievements, a job well done, being a good provider, being successful, having a great body or a nice car.

Like most people, you may have listed things such as people acknowledging me, completing a successful task, my career, my community work, my body or my relationship. If so, ask yourself this question: is this self-esteem or external esteem?

Anything that gives you confidence and esteem from outside is external esteem. If you rely on your esteem coming from your bank balance, your looks, your success in the world, your family or your car, you are relying on external esteem. These things are all subject to change. By nature of them being in the world of change, they are not strictly real. Properties and estates that were once in the hands of famous people are now in the hands of completely different families. Look at the world map. In the last three hundred years we have seen countries disappear, new countries arise and borders change. When you affix your esteem onto something that can change, you run the risk of your sense of esteem changing.

Now, there's nothing wrong with getting a kick out of your success in the world. It is natural and human to want to succeed. However, if you pin your self-worth to the external, you are placing yourself on a foundation with wobbly supports.

What is true self-esteem? The answer is in the words: esteem from your self, your Spirit. It is the *direct experience* of who you are. Direct experience takes you out of the realm of theory and brings you to experiencing your being or your Self.

Your being or Spirit is a presence that you experience as ancient and timeless. It is without personality — it merely is. It is vast, unlimited and permanent. It never dies and time does not touch it. Its only desire is to reconnect with the Divine Force. If you perceive yourself as your identity and behaviour, these begin to shroud your Spirit and you forget who you really are. If you think of your various identities as a series of wrappings around your Spirit, after a while, the light shining from your Spirit will become dull.

The identities that have the strongest hold over you are the ones that you are not aware of. They are the ones that you have had for so long that you don't even notice them anymore. It is like someone who wears a funny hat to a party. The longer they wear it, the more likely they are to forget that they have it on. Everybody else at the party notices, but for the person wearing the hat it has just become an extension of themselves.

It is through your personality that you relate to other humans. This is how you play the game of life on the physical plane. Without your personality, there would be no game, no interaction. There would be nothing to talk about, but problems arise when you believe your personality is the sum total of who you are.

RECLAIMING YOUR THRONE

A monarch once ruled a vast kingdom. One day as he sat on his throne he came up with a novel idea. "Wouldn't it be fascinating", he thought to himself, "to travel my kingdom as an ordinary person." He decided to put on common clothes and walk through the land to see what the world looked like from a commoner's perspective. As he exchanged his royal clothes for peasant attire, a strange thing happened. The clothes had a mesmerising effect. He began to forget his royal heritage and started believing he was a commoner.

For years the monarch wandered the length and breadth of the kingdom. He had many amazing experiences and met some fascinating people, yet in the back of his mind there was always some nagging suspicion that something was not quite right. It was as if there was some memory he could not recall. He felt as if he was missing something and yet he could not determine what it was.

Meanwhile, the kingdom itself was in disarray. Without the strong calming presence of the monarch, people were lost and confused.

One day, as the monarch walked along a country road, this feeling of something missing became particularly strong. He came around a bend and spotted a quiet pond within a glade of trees. Feeling weary, he sat for a while in this quiet little sanctuary. As he looked into the still waters of the pond he saw his own reflection. The face looking back at him was travel worn. He could see etched into that face all his experiences from his years on the road. As he looked into his own eyes, he suddenly saw something very different. Behind his eyes was a presence that was greater and more enduring than all his experiences. In that instant he was able to see his true self. All the memories came flooding back as he realised that all along he had been regent of a huge kingdom.

This is the true spiritual quest. Like the monarch, you need to return to the throne so that your kingdom once more takes on its true grandeur.

THE SPIRIT'S TOOLKIT

ACCESSING YOUR SPIRIT

The only way to experience true freedom is to live in touch with your own Spirit. Suffering or discontent come to you through the body, mind or emotions. The body can feel pain, the mind can become cluttered, and the emotions of grief, sadness or despair can flood you. The soul or spirit by its nature feels only its magnificence.

There are three keys to preparing yourself for a life where the experience of Spirit is the dominant force: surrender, acting on Divine Will and achieving inner silence.

SURRENDER

Surrender is the state of being content with your circumstances in life. Surrender comes when you place no demands on what you need in order to be happy. The key is understanding the difference between choice and demand.

A choice refers to a situation occurring that would be preferable to you. A demand is having a particular desire and only being happy if that desire comes to fruition.

Let's say that you want to travel overseas on a holiday. Your choice is to travel on a certain date. If for some reason you cannot travel on this date, your equanimity is undisturbed. However, if you demand that you must travel on that date then your happiness will be dictated by external factors.

Perhaps your choice is to move into a new, luxurious home. If it remains a choice you are still able to enjoy where you are living. If it becomes a demand, then your happiness is dictated by whether or not you can move into your new home.

Recently I was surfing on the island of Bali. The surf was particularly large and I was using one of my favourite surfboards. It was a limited edition board shaped by one of the best surfboard builders in the world. After a particularly powerful wipe-out, the leash on my board snapped and the board washed on to the beach. As I was swimming in after my board, someone ran down the beach, picked up my board and ran off with it!

Years ago if this had happened to me I would have been devastated because internally I would have demanded that a situation like this "should not have happened". However, the event had happened. I could not change it. But surrender does not mean giving up. My choice was to find my surfboard. After exploring all avenues to recover it, I realised that it was gone for good. I felt at the time that my happiness was not dependant on reclaiming the board, and I was able to let the incident go.

It is the desired demands which come through your mind that create restlessness or suffering. When you are attached to an outcome, and that outcome doesn't pan out, it begins to create a tension in you. On one side is the reality of what is happening, and on the other side is what you *want* to happen. You may not look like the kid in the playground who can't get their own way, but essentially that's how you feel.

Does this mean that you should not desire anything of this world? Should you just sit in an armchair and never do anything? No, of course not. You were placed here for many reasons. You have to set your course on the ship of life and head full tilt in that direction. That's being focussed — going full steam ahead for your outcome, being completely committed but not attached to it. It is the great spiritual paradox — wanting without wanting. Desiring without desiring. When you attach too much to an outcome it can blind you to what is in your best interests.

A small child may beg and plead with you to let them have that giant bag of candy. They believe in all their heart that if they could have it they would be satisfied. As their desire grows, they become more and more frustrated and unhappy. They *know* if only they could have the whole bag they would be happy. Looking from your higher vantage point, you know that if they eat the whole bag they'll probably be sick.

Your mind is the child and your Spirit is the adult who lovingly denies you the candy because it is looking after your best interests. Your mind or human will believes it knows best what will make you happy. Your Spirit or your Divine will, however, holds the key to your true happiness.

HUMAN WILL AND DIVINE WILL

Your Spirit interfaces with your personality through the intuition of the Sage. Your intuition is your Divine guidance telling you where to go and what to do. Human will, on the other hand, is the will driven by the desires of the mind, much like the example I used of the child driven to eat the whole bag of candy. When you act on human will, you act out of your individual consciousness. When you act on Divine Will, you move in concert with the entire universe.

When I look back on my life, I thank God that certain things I desperately wanted never came to fruition. I realise that in the long run they would have made me unhappy. I also realise that when I was in that state of quiet desperation I wasn't really listening to my own inner guidance or intuition. I was acting out of "I want . . ."

I also see things that I didn't want, things that I wished would have gone away, times when I was unhappy. I look back and see everyone of those times as a blessing, as leading me somewhere, trying to teach me something.

It often seems to me that there are two partners on the dance floor of our lives: our individual personality and our Spirit. We experience suffering and unrest when the personality dominates the Spirit and they are dancing completing out of sync: the personality wants to go one way and the Spirit the other. It is as if a beautiful orchestra is playing, the Spirit is swaying in rhapsody to its song, and the personality, only vaguely aware of the music, is chatting away about their busy day at work. It is definitely not a harmonious pair.

I have always liked the saying, "Feet on the ground and head in the stars." To me, this means getting the personality and the Spirit to dance in harmony. The personality needs to serve the Spirit in order to be happy. When the personality is trying to dominate the Spirit by blocking its natural direction, unhappiness is the only result. When the personality aligns with the Spirit it creates a powerful force.

INNER SILENCE

> *"I found I had less and less to say, until finally, I became silent, and began to listen. I discovered in the silence, the voice of God."*
>
> SOREN KIERKEGAARD

Rene Descartes was famous for uttering in the seventeenth century, "I think, therefore I am." With respect to Monsieur Descartes, I believe that to discover who you are, you have to do the exact opposite. You have to stop thinking.

Have you ever sat next to a lake and gazed at your own reflection? Sometimes as you sit there watching yourself, a slight breeze comes and ruffles the surface. In an instant your reflection becomes distorted. As the wind grows, the reflection becomes more distorted and eventually disappears completely.

It is exactly the same in terms of having a sense of yourself. If your mind is slightly disturbed, your "picture" of who you are will be distorted. If your thinking is turbulent, you will completely lose your sense of who you are. You may even confuse yourself with your thoughts, believing that your thought process is who you are.

The mind is used to travelling outward, thinking and planning, either in the past or in the future. It is rarely in the present. The key is to live in the stillness of the present so that you can see your own reflection. That reflection is who you really are, and is more beautiful than any work of art you will find in the finest gallery.

TRAITS THAT SELF-SABOTAGE

THE HIDDEN TRAP

You cannot overdevelop Spirit. There is no such thing as being too much in touch with your true self. However, my experience is that those who focus only on this fifth element cannot sustain it. Sometimes people mistake the messages of their mind as directions from their Spirit. They abandon their families and friends and seek an escapist reality. If you abandon all your responsibilities then you are abandoning what your Spirit wants you to do on this physical plane. You are in essence abandoning your Spirit.

The first four elements — the Visionary Leader, Achiever, Poet and Sage — provide a platform from which the rocketship of the Spirit can take off. Just as you need a platform to launch a rocket, so you need a base on which to build your spiritual life. You need to embrace the first four elements to sustain your spiritual quest.

You need to obey the rules of the physical plane of where you live. If you believe that as a Spirit you are unlimited and that gravity no longer applies to you, then you're probably in for a few bruises. If you ignore the first four elements, then you may also encounter some injuries. Just as there is gravity, so is there fire, earth, water and air. The earth provides a solid grounding for your Visionary Leader to give you stability. Fire provides the energy and passion of your Achiever to fulfil your vision. Water allows the creativity of your Poet to flow, and air enables your Sage to reach expanded viewpoints.

Having all of the first four elements gives you balance within yourself and the ability to live a balanced life. The first four elements allow you to create a container that is strong enough to hold the presence of your Spirit. Imagine filling a container with liquid gold. If that container has cracks in it or is strong in some places and weak in others, will it be able to hold this precious commodity?

I have met many people who singularly pursue the spiritual life. Deep down they are discontent because the rest of their life is unfulfilled. Many of these people attempt to use spirituality as some sort of escape, as a way of fleeing from their present unhappiness. Trying to escape is a violation of your Spirit. You are here on this plane to learn certain lessons, not run away from them. The whole idea is to surrender to what your Spirit wants for you.

The pursuit of true spirituality requires a lot of courage because you have to face all the blocks that stand in the way of becoming who you really are. Without combining all five elements, the journey becomes very difficult.

Arriving at your own Quintessence is perhaps the greatest gift you can give to yourself and the world.

PART THREE

AWAKENING THE ELEMENTS

Awakening the elements is a process of allowing what is inside you to emerge.

You have to remember that all your elements sit inside you. When you look at a bodybuilder who has transformed their body into a huge mass, you might think they have grown more muscles. However, exactly the same number of muscle fibres were there when they were a ninety pound weakling. All they did was expand those fibres. It is the same with your elemental makeup — it is already there, a natural part of your psyche. In fact, it is not possible to function on this plane of existence without at least a small portion of these five elements. In awakening the elements, you simply grow and expand them.

To awaken these aspects of yourself, all you have to do is unlock the door. Many people have actually closed and locked the door on certain elements of who they naturally are. There are numerous factors that determine why somebody closes the door in the first place — the culture they grow up in, family conditioning and fear of being ridiculed, to name just a few. However, rather than focusing too much on why this happens, it is more productive to just wake up that part of you.

THE STEPS TO AWAKENING

"The ancestor of every action is a thought."

RALPH WALDO EMERSON.

Steps 1 and 2 apply to all of the five elements. Steps 3 and 4 apply only to the first four elements.

STEP 1: COMMITMENT

You absolutely have to want to awaken your Visionary Leader, Achiever, Poet, Sage and Spirit. An idle interest is not going to be effective. You have to want to be a person who is powerful, inspirational and committed to their unique vision and commit yourself to becoming that person. All of this brings certain responsibilities to fulfil yourself and your vision.

STEP 2: INTENTION

Intention is the precursor of all things, and it is the most important and effective process to awaken all of the five elements. Intend that your elements are waking up. Start with one element at a time. Using your intuition, select an element that you feel would help you become more successful or integrated. Say, for example, that you feel that you are holding yourself back in life because you haven't awakened your Visionary Leader. Use the committed force of your mind to intend that your Visionary Leader will awaken. Intend that you become a Visionary Leader. Don't underestimate the power of your own intended will. I have seen many people who have used this one process and experienced a tremendous change in their life.

A friend of mine recognised that what was missing in himself was his inner Sage. He passionately intended that his Sage awaken. The change within him was profound. Within a few months people began seeking him out to ask for his assistance and guidance. His inner wisdom and intuition dramatically increased. Just by intending this one element to awaken, he automatically embraced the qualities of the Sage.

If you want to lift a book from a shelf, you first need to intend it. If you want to sail around the world you first need to intend it. If you want to go to the shop to buy a loaf of bread, you first need to intend it. Intention is seeing and feeling what you want and deciding that this will happen. It is a conscious choice to have what you want.

Intention is the mother of all actions. Step 2 is about intending your elements to waken, arise and bloom. That's the key. Just intend it happening. The elements are already there inside you, but you have to *want* to awaken them. This intention has to come from a deep commitment. Once you have that commitment, just intend the awakening. You have to want it. Visualise this power awakening.

After intending the elements to awaken, let your subconscious mind and the Divine Force do their work. Let them look after the details.

STEP 3: CLEARING AWAY JUDGEMENT

Step 3 involves recognising the obstacles or blocks that stand in the way of awakening the Visionary Leader, the Achiever, the Poet and the Sage.

Step 3 is a bit like cleaning a room. To begin, you need to see what in the room needs cleaning. It would be very difficult to clean a room blindfolded. If you specialised in denial and said, "there's nothing in this room to clean up", you would be completely ineffective. It is the same with "cleaning up" yourself. You need to look at the very things that stand in the way of your evolution. You need to recognise what the obstacles are that prevent you from embracing all the elements.

The primary obstacles are your own beliefs or judgements about what you perceive to be the negative tendencies of the first four elements. You see, it is very difficult to make a commitment to something that you consider bad or wrong. If you subconsciously believed, for example, that having an intimate relationship would eventually lead to heartbreak, then you might find that you constantly have one foot on the brakes in relationships.

In the following exercise, the focus is on changing your thoughts so that you can effect change in your outward behaviour.

All your actions are derived from your thoughts. The difference between people's behaviours originates from their thinking. Someone who is a "career criminal", for example, has an entirely different thinking pattern to someone who has integrity.

Generally speaking, the more judgements you have on any element, the more that element will be suppressed. You need to listen to your negative judgements to become aware of the blocks that stand in your way and also to determine which elements you need to awaken.

JUDGEMENTS ABOUT THE VISIONARY LEADER

To give you an example, following are some of the negative judgements people may have about the Visionary Leader:

controlling
egotistical
arrogant
power driven
show off
manipulative
domineering
bossy
tyrannical
corrupt

Do you share any of these negative judgements? Do you have any others? If so, jot them down next to this list. (If you don't have a pen make the list in your head.) Don't write anything "nice," you are looking for the blocks.

JUDGEMENTS ABOUT THE ACHIEVER

Some people believe Achievers are:

pushy
ruthless

blinkered
manic
workaholic
abusive
driven

In the space next to these words add any other negative judgements that you might have about the Achiever (or make the list in your head). Again, don't write anything "nice", you are looking for the obstacles.

JUDGEMENTS ABOUT THE POET

The following are the most common judgments people have about the Poet:

weak
dreamy
unrealistic
selfish
indulgent
unproductive
soft
self-obsessed

If you can think of other negative impressions of the Poet, write them down or mentally list them.

JUDGEMENTS ABOUT THE SAGE

When people think about the Sage, they sometimes come up with the following judgements:

critical
self-important
deluded
aloof
flakey
superior
strange
weird

Do any of these ring a bell? If you have more, add them to the list.

THE JUDGEMENT PROCESS

Now that you have your lists, circle the words that you think are true. Say, for example, you look at the Visionary Leader list and think, "Well yes, they definitely are arrogant." What you have found is an "absolute". You believe that attribute is absolutely true.

If you look at the Achiever's list and think, "Well yes, Achievers definitely are abusive." you have found an absolute. You believe it is *absolutely* true.

If you really believe that all Visionary Leaders are domineering and arrogant, your subconscious mind would do everything in its power to prevent you from becoming a Visionary Leader as you would be frightened, by association, of becoming arrogant and domineering. If you thought Sages were flakey or Poets were weak, then you would not feel deeply attracted to developing these elements.

DEALING WITH ABSOLUTES

To overcome these absolutes or negative judgements, ask yourself, "Is it really true that all Visionary Leaders are arrogant (or show offs, egocentric, etc.)?"

Begin going through your lists and ask yourself if your judgements pertain to *all* Visionary Leaders, *all* Achievers, *all* Poets, *all* Sages. If, for example, you can think of just one Visionary Leader who does not have these negative qualities, then your absolute is no longer absolute. If you can find one Sage who isn't flakey, then it is also not an absolute. Doing this helps undermine your negative judgements and takes away their power over you.

Remember, it is difficult to have what you judge. Judgements are thoughts. Thoughts carry great power and shape who we are. I knew someone who deep down absolutely believed that all rich people were evil. Needless to say he was always broke.

STEP 4: FOCUSING ON THE QUALITIES

In each of the first four elements there are two primary qualities. These are:

The Visionary Leader—Purpose and Power
The Achiever—Commitment and Action
The Poet—Having an Open Heart and Appreciation
The Sage—Intuition and Perceiving Alternative Realities

All the other qualities in an element will flow from the two primary attributes. For example, in the Visionary Leader, the quality of inspiration will emanate from Purpose and Power. Great leaders who inspire themselves and others have a purpose, and the personal power to convey that purpose. Winston Churchill galvanized Britain into the single purpose of maintaining their freedom in the Second World War. His personal power inspired a nation to resist the seemingly impossible onslaught of the third Reich.

If you look at Martin, the Native American medicine man mentioned in the Sage chapter, you can see the reason he is such an extraordinary Sage. He has a high degree of mastery in the two primary qualities: Intuition and Perceiving Alternative Realities.

You can awaken an element within you by focusing on the two primary qualities. If you want to become more of an Achiever, begin by focusing on bringing more Commitment and Action into your life. You can also use the techniques found in this book, particularly in the Toolkit section of each element, to help you attain more of the two primary qualities. For example, using the "Gratitude" exercise can help open your heart, while the "Walking with Fresh Eyes" exercise can be a very powerful method to increase your sense of appreciation. I remember one person telling me that this particular exercise changed his life. It had awakened within him a sense of wonder at seeing the inherent beauty of the world. He felt as if his world went from shades of grey to vibrant colour.

A PERSONAL NOTE

As I conclude this book, I want to thank you, the reader, for embarking on this journey with me. I truly hope that within these pages you have found some tools to make your life's journey an extraordinary experience.

I know that the 5 elements have been an invaluable star in which to steer my boat. There always seem to be new lessons for me to learn and I often have to remind myself to stay in balance with all 5 elements.

Personally, my life always works best when I place my spiritual life in the top priority. The times when I have failed to do this, always seem to produce a feeling of hollowness within me, no matter how successful I have been.

I feel that God or the Divine Force is the source of all things. I know that personal change comes more easily when we embrace this Force.

I wish you well on your journey and leave you with one of my favourite passages by Tennyson, that speak of a greater reality, that we can all share.

"Moreover, something is or seems,
That touches me with mystic gleams,
Like glimpses of forgotten dreams –
Of something felt, of something here;
Of something done, I know not where;
Such as no language may declare."

About the Author

Thousands of people and major corporations have attended Brendan Nichols' dynamic and far-reaching seminars.

In 1976 Brendan travelled to India to study Eastern Philosophy at a spiritual retreat. Here he learned a meditation technique, which has become a practice to this day.

In the 1980's he became a leading troubleshooter in the field of Real Estate project marketing. His company achieved such outstanding accomplishments such as: every sales person in the company being in the top 1% of producers in the country and spearheading the sales on one of the first true environmental estates.

He worked extensively, for 6 years, with Robert Kiyosaki (author of Rich Dad Poor Dad), the former president of the Excellerated Learning Institute in the USA and became Kiyosaki's first fully trained Australian presenter, delivering business and personal development seminars in the United States, Australia and New Zealand. He was one of only 6 instructors ever to be certified from the 40,000 graduates that attended the Institute's courses.

While teaching these seminars in New Zealand, he was publicly honored by the Maori people who gave him the title of Rangatira (an elder or chief). An extremely rare honor for an outsider.

For two years in succession, Brendan was the only non-indigenous teacher invited to host and teach at Corroboree, a world wide meeting of indigenous people. He worked with Wallace Black Elk one of the most revered Native American Elders, about whom the book "The Sacred Ways of a Lakota" was written. Black Elk personally selected him as the only representative at Corroborree to continue his teachings.

He has researched most of the success and motivational literature and studied the methods and effects of Gestalt therapy, twelve step groups, inner child therapy, voice dialogue, bodywork therapies, NLP, dynamic expression, holotropic breathing, addictions work and psychology.

His extensive knowledge and inner clarity has led to the creation of a highly effective system that produces powerful positive change.

His seminars are highly inspirational. They focus on being successful in the spiritual and material world.

Creating the Life of Your Dreams Video

With Brendan Nichols

In this 45 minute video presentation captured by a professional film crew, we take you inside one of Brendan's seminars. You will find the essential ingredients to live the life of your dreams; blending a successful life with spiritual fulfilment.

Discover:

- How to identify what is the life of your dreams.
- What is the state of Totality and how does it affect everything you do.
- Why it is crucial to live with purpose.
- The two things you need to open your heart, have fulfiling relation ships and enjoy life.
- The key to unlocking your intuitive power.
- How the principle of surrender creates inner peace and fulfilment.

Filled with powerful anecdotes, stories, warmth and humour this video is entertaining and inspirational.
Available in Australian or American format.
$34.95 AUD / $29.95 USA plus shipping

TO ORDER: Phone 1 300 8888 13 or 61 2 9977 5064
E- Mail www.brendannichols.com
Write PO BOX 1227
Manly 2095 Australia

Also available

Audio Cassette Seri

By Brendan Nichol

Free Internet Newsletter

Please visit our website,

www.brendannichols.com

to:

- Register for our free internet newsletter, released every two months. The newsletter is designed to enhance your life and lift your spirit.
- On the website you will also find articles and information about our products.
- You can also locate Brendan Nichols schedule if you wish to experience one of his life changing seminars.